LUIGI CARAMII
MARIANNA SASSO

ISCHIA, the island of cinematography: a sociological study on its societal development

Translated from the Italian by
Anna G. Di Meglio

To my dear father, who successfully passed on to me and my sister a profound and sentimental love for Ischia, his beloved native island. It is thanks to him that we are proud of our Ischitan culture and Neapolitan heritage.

Anna G. Di Meglio

Luigi Caramiello is credited with authoring the Introduction, The Conclusion and Chapters 1,2,4. Marianna Sasso is credited with authoring Chapters 3 and 5.

ISBN: 979-86-484-2813-3

©*2020 by Luigi Caramiello and Marianna Sasso*

All rights reserved. No part of this document may be reproduced or transmitted in any form or by any means, electronic, mechanical, photocopying, recording, or otherwise, without prior written permission of Luigi Caramiello and Marianna Sasso.

Table of contents

Introduction

Chapter I. Ischia's Social Imaginary
1.1 A "Discovered" Island
1.2 Pithecusa's Past
1.3 The Indigenous Look
1.4 The Island's Location

Chapter II: The Age of the First Movie Theatre. The Island during the Period of Italian Unification.

2.1 "Cinema Unione": The Dreams of the Ischitans
2.2 The Problem of Monoculture: The Ischitan Vine Variety
2.3 Customs and Traditions: The 'Carusiello' Ballad
2.4 "Merecoppe": Memories of Everyday Life
2.5 Lacco Ameno: Fishing and Crafts
2.6 The Terracotta Fishermen
2.7 The Opening of the Theatres: The Islanders Go to the Movies

Chapter III: Crews arrive on the Island. Directors and actors come to Ischia

3.1 Dreams of Motion-Picture Films
3.2 The Neorealist island
3.3 The Caribbean Gulf: The Island of the Pirates
3.3.1 Dispersed Films
3.4 The Island of Horrors
3.5 The Island of Crime Drama: The Mongibello by Patricia Highsmith
3.6 Blockbuster Ischia: "Cleopatra"
3.7 The Island is Promoted
    3.7.1 The Adventures of Cineriz
    3.7.2 When When Will You Come…To Ischia?
    3.7.3 A Footnote on Sound. Ischia and Songs.
3.8 The Supermarket Island

Chapter IV. The Take-Off Begins. Industrialists and Intellectuals: An Identical Love.
4.1 The Strategies of Innovation
    4.1.1 The Dilemmas of Modernization: Identity and Nostalgia
4.2 Underdevelopment and Arcadia: Visconti's Poetry and Rizzoli's Plans
4.3 The Island of Il Gattopardo: Luchino Visconti
4.4 Rizzoli's Plans
4.5 The Passion of a Self-Made Man
    4.5.1 The Knight Commander Remembered by Great Writers
    4.5.2 A Trusted Technician: Stories Told by a Foreman

Chapter V: The New Presence of Cinema in Ischia
5.1 The Spotlights Turn on Again
5.2 Epomeo: Ciak is Filmed
5.3 Festivals Return to Ischia
5.4 The Foreign Film Festival
5.5 Ischia Global & Music Film Festival
    5.5.1 The Testimony of the President of the Accademia Internazionale Arte-Ischia

CONCLUSIONS

BIBLIOGRAPHICAL REFERENCES

CONSULTED WEBSITES

FILMOGRAPHY

THE ANGELO RIZZOLI AWARD FOR CINEMATOGRAPHERS

In this beautiful book about Ischia and its development within the tourism industry, Caramiello and Sasso examine the way in which the world of cinematography caused and sustained the green island's transformation from a rural and impoverished area to one that is modern and touristic. It is about a historic and sociological sequence of events that was probably never investigated before with such care to an abundance of details. The movie industry is indeed at the core of the transformation; not only did it help in garnering remarkable moments on the island but also in being the bearer of an entrepreneurial culture that up to that time was unknown to Ischia and the rest of Southern Italy.

Caramiello and Sasso's book is therefore not one of the typical local "biographies" of which our country is rich. Instead, it is something very different and more. It is a study of social changes and, in particular, of the social, economic and cultural factors that can set off the development and modernization of a community.

It is what one generally calls "a case study", a study that aims to understand the dynamics of the transformation of a specific social environment, namely the causes that are at the base of the stagnation or of the progress of a community, of the immobilism or of the vitality of a social community.

Gerardo Ragone

Introduction

This work proposes to offer a clear and comprehensible research study aimed at explaining the interest for cinematography on the island of Ischia as well as ancient Pithecusa's inhabitants' reaction to the film industry's impact on the social, cultural and economic dimensions of the island.

Ischia expresses an "island-type" of dimension that is quite characteristic not only because its economy was never based on the fishing industry (a characteristic that is common to other Southern islands), but because of the nature of its inhabitants' daily life. Traditionally agriculturists (at least up to the time that tourism exploded on the island), these inhabitants always lived in a particularly beautiful environment which was at the same time unstable, precarious, dangerous; a land undergoing continual changes and movements due to its volcanic nature.

It is known that the charm of the people, like that of the places, often gets overlooked by logical analyses and is almost never ascribable solely to rational assessments. It is for this reason that the enchanting beaches, the picturesque corners, and the impressive sea crevices alone do not do the island justice when describing its charm. Probably the distinctiveness of this place was created by a magical combination between environment and social system. It's a bit the way Truman Capote wrote: *Living on an island is after all like living in a still ship at sea, perennially anchored* (Cf. Di Costanzo, 2000, p.203) and to succeed at making this very idea of isolation the reason for growth is undoubtedly valuable, although primordial.

Going beyond one's limits and "evading" from one's physical confines and from those of one's own mentality and culture are catalysts at the base of every developing civilization. Societies construct and cement their identity through *the social imaginary*. Myths and fairy tales have a common "explanation" that sometimes is dragged right into the contemporary world (Cf. Campbell, 2007). Short stories and legends, some which share an origin too, often express identical meanings; present in every population, in some way they reflect history (Cf., Braudel, 1987; Rossi Doria, 1990; Toynbee, 2003). All of this aside, particular environmental phenomena tied to volcanism were unexplainable in the minds of the island's first inhabitants; this ensured that fantastic tales would develop about the island, about its form, about the geographical location of its sites. Tales that were more captivating and appealing than those of other places, fascinating to the point that their memory would be rooted in the extraordinary Homeric tales. The legendary fabrications and narrations that followed, as well as their widespread historical diffusion, contributed quite a bit to making Ischia one of the most visited islands of the Mediterranean. Throughout the centuries, a rich realm of wonder formed gradually. It was a dimension of the memory, a place in one's soul if you will, that favoured inspiration in every type of artist.

It was inevitable that the new mythology of "technological images" would also attract Ischia. The character of media science in modern times and the advent of communication sciences (Cf., Morcellini, Fatelli, 1995) maintain a fundamental tie with the history of cinema and its evolution. We will see that even the green island and its characteristic development must have contracted their conspicuous debt with the world of celluloid.

In 1936, teams of technicians and artists landed on the green island to shoot their first films. The positive attitude of the people in response to this was immediately noticed. Many island inhabitants were involved in various productions, not only as suppliers and producers of goods and services but also as people offering a personal artistic contribution as extras. A bit for necessity's sake and a bit for fun, the local community became detached from its old habits and ancestral traditional rituals and instead suddenly became projected amongst the infinite games of the new "factory of dreams". It was in this fashion that even Ischia made its entrance into the modern world. It entered via the main door, in the mass sanctuary that was the most exclusive one of contemporary mythology: the movies.

The binomial "Cinema-Ischia" was born this way; it was a term that witnessed the greater splendours during the years of the island's "boom" such as the temple of high-society and the international Jet-Set. In other words, it was the era of Angelo Rizzoli, Luchino Visconti, Liz Taylor, Richard Burton, Burt Lancaster, Romy Schneider and many other "protagonists" of the "Ischitan scene" of the postwar period of World War II (these were just a few amongst the most famous ones).

The research agenda's development is based on several directives:

-to understand how the island became a filming location (or rather, an appropriate and effective setting for the production of the most diverse cinematographic products) and in what way this "promotional" mechanism, activated at various levels, formed a determining, propellant factor in the development and "modernization" process of this emblematic Southern reality.

-to understand--through the analysis of various cinematographic products realized over the years--to what degree the movie industry represented the island's reality, how the island was promoted through cinematographic productions of Cineriz and others, and whether or not Ischia's territory was only used in a "technical" sense, easily providing a setting with marvellous views.

-to highlight--through the examination of the islanders' past--how the movie industry, since its inception, became an integral part of the islanders' lives both as an opportunity for entertainment and socialization and as a resource of easy earnings which was no less than fun.

-to give a voice to the islanders' direct testimonials and to their collective memories. Since research cannot avail itself exclusively of facts from documented sources, an attempt is made to discover what has remained in the islanders from those experiences and what they have gained, in all regards. The reflection on the subject at hand also refers to sociological literature, in general, and that concerning the movie industry, as well as cultural and communicative processes. Moreover, this work avails itself of the consultation of books, articles, investigations and much more material published by specialized magazines and the movie industry.

-to show how this island was the object of a deep love that brought together two fundamental celebrities of the post-war Italian movie industry: Angelo Rizzoli and Luchino Visconti.

The book concludes with an effective overview of the new initiatives in the cultural field and specifically in the movie industry, all actually of interest on the island. The overview helps one understand how much this interest, these "movements" in action, can be considered indications of an authentic productive relaunch in the movie industry; in other words, they are real signals afoot of new constructive experiences, after a long period of stasis and silence.

CHAPTER 1: Ischia Seen Through the Social Imaginary

1.1 A 'Discovered' Island

The island of Ischia, a destination of various types of visitors, has always been one of the most desired sites of tourists and globe-trotters. The interest that the island is able to raise most definitely derives from its unmatchable beauty: the chestnut trees that cover the flanks of Mount Epomeo, the impressive pine forest of the Arso, the thick scrub of Caruso....these all represent the most evident factors of its characteristic landscape, thereby making this island incomparable and conferring upon it a captivating, rustic flavour almost as if it were a promise of Arcadia.
In the same fashion, the medicinal potential of its thermal springs, therapeutic mud, eerie charm of fumaroles, along with beautiful beaches, the cozy ravines, majestic promontories, the many creeks, increase its charm and lure. Its position in the Gulf of Naples also includes a picture of extraordinary richness and dramatic intensity (Malagoli, 1987). But, in addition to the undeniable beauty of the natural scenery, what else has contributed to the attractiveness of this island? Why has Ischia been the territory of choice for the world of cinema? Why has it been chosen as the setting for many filmmakers' shootings? Ischia, has always been a name that evokes myths, magic, memories and places that have always interested the cinema world. The lava mass spills, which occurred several times from the bottom of the Tyrrhenian Sea, gave birth thousands and thousands of years ago to this delightful island whose volcanic and geological evolution characterize its alternating eruptions and periods of quiescence. Ever since the last volcanic phenomena occurring between

1301 and 1305, the Arso lava flow, and the earthquakes of Casamicciola of 1881-1883, volcanism seems to occur only in a benign manner, especially through the heat of several thermal springs on the island (AX, 1864).

The ancients, failing to explain these phenomena, gave wide scope for imagination, creating numerous legends linked to the size of the places (Cf., Hillman, 2004) which, in their simplicity and candor, have contributed to enrich the island's charm (Deuringer, 1959). A myth says that one of the Titans defeated by Jupiter, the giant Typhon, plummeted beneath the island of Ischia which the Head of Olympus hurled over him so that he would atone for his wrongdoings. Typhon attempted to defend himself by hitting him with a rock which, according to legend, would be the current Mushroom of Lacco Ameno. But the giant was defeated and imprisoned under the island, in the bowels of Mount Epomeo. The classic myth has been variously reworked by tradition. In fact, a "popular" version of the legend tells that some of Typhon's limbs were scattered throughout the island.

The most characteristic names of some of the island's locations would be the equivalent of the names of the body parts of the mythical hero: *Ciglio 'eyelash', Panza 'belly', Testaccio 'big head'*, are some examples. Even *Il Fungo* "the mushroom", in popular imagination, is supposedly a giant body part that modesty forbids us to mention. In the classic version, the imprisoned Titan endured his harsh punishment for a long time until he finally asked that Venus Cytherea ask Jupiter to forgive him. Hot tears were flowing from the eyes of the repentant rebel, like a fountain ('Fontana', the name of another island location) and Zeus, moved to compassion, forgave him turning his tears into thermal waters (Cf. Di Meglio, b1987). So, the Titan Typhon, protagonist of a major Mediterranean myth, collapses in Anatolia, then ends up in Etna's magma, and is finally forced to hold up the island of Ischia (Cf., Vuoso, 2002).

The "discovery" of the island is ancient: when the gods arrived to Ischia, they loved to guzzle there. Ulysses was a guest of the King of the Phaeacians, Alcinous, on the Hill of Castiglioni; Aphrodite, Goddess of beauty, used to immerse himself in its thermal waters; and in the Christian context, the Archangel Michael made an appearance here and gave a name to the famous highpoint: Sant'Angelo.

Over time, the versions of the various legends have multiplied, whether passed down orally or in written form, transmitted from generation to generation, enriched with new details (Deuringer, 1959). At the dawn of modernity, the 'scientific representations' of the island were added to its fantastic and mythical representations. An important and tangible graphical reconstruction of the island was the first topographic map, created by Mario Cartaro from Viterbo. The map was a masterpiece of cartography of the late 1500s which tried to connote all the peculiarities of the site, defining the boundaries and distances with respectable approximations, at least considering the parameters of that time period. This map was attached to the medical book written and published in 1588 by the naturalist Julius Iasolino, *"De rimedi naturali che sono nell'isola di Pithecusa, oggi della Ischia"* (*"The natural remedies that are on the island of Pithecusa, today called Ischia"*), a work that describes all the therapeutic virtues of the island's waters. Thanks to the circulation of the book, even Ischia's image began to become known in Europe and the world (Iasolino, 1588). It is in this manner that Ischia associates to its fantastic and fairy-tale identity a rigorous and detailed image of its character and vocational dimension, heading along this path to establish itself as the place of well-being and delight that we know these days.

The island, through myths and legends, has become a peculiar imaginary territory, a place that even before it was recognized as a true and real representation in the figurative sense, is a psychic and conceptual landscape, a way of thinking about reality (De Seta, 1982). From the moment that collective imagination and the tourist culture--always looking for curiosities and distinctive traits--let themselves be seduced by the oral tales, also very impressive are the many testaments that you can obtain in person from the "old" inhabitants, such being the imaginative stories told by taxi drivers and boaters. The story of "Constantine the pirate" is distinctive. He is a simple sailor who was called upon to be an extra in the film "Il corsaro dell'isola verde" (*"The privateer of the green island"*) and then becomes a celebrity of the place, a real attraction for tourists, as he reintroduces to them in a very original manner the atmosphere of that time. The "pirate" islander, skillfully using his wooden leg (which was actually lost in an accident before the film) and black bandana over his left eye, becomes a very characteristic figure of Ischitan folklore through his stories and anecdotes (Cf., Vuoso, 2002). But, when talking about the local fauna, we cannot ignore the role of the boatman Don Mimi and many others, who, skirting the island with their boats, show tourists the many gorges, rock formations, and cliffs of diverse and bizarre formations--assumedly due to erosion, landslides, and earthquakes throughout the ages—and strain to see in such forms particular figures, shapes, objects, and animals. In reality, one is playing a bit with the imagination of the visitors by using the same lytic formations that the Swiss psychiatrist Rorschach used in his inkblots to fathom the personality of his patients. It is perhaps an odd but certainly effective way to give an identity, a value, a meaning, even to the most hidden or ordinary parts of the territory, and a way to arouse the interest and participation of travelers. This little game had already begun in the 1960s, and had among its main players the many film actors with whom the boatmen would roam along the stunning coastline.

The rocks have therefore taken on the strangest names: Mussolini's head, a majestic elephant, even Christ's foot with an attached nail (for others it is the foot of Maradona, which is still somehow the foot "de dios"), and many other images that are "identified", just like when you look at the clouds while passing time and looking at tourists. To these impressive ambiances is added a feeling that is not easily expressed in words, as it is a deep emotion. It is also this place's ability to fascinate that has attracted many notable cinematographic productions on site.

The island has in fact exercised its fascination as of ancient times, and in a manner so intense and multi-faceted so as to catch the interest of writers, men of thought, and artists, to name a few. There are many very distinguished writers who have drawn inspiration from this land to create or provide a setting for their works. It is a territory that has at times even been capable of changing opinions and tastes, as was the case with Nietsche, who after his stay in Ischia cut off his collaboration with Wagner, a somber, austere person that was ill-suited to the sun that the island had impressed on his soul and that he instead rediscovered in the magic offered by Bizet's opera practically unbeknownst to him: Carmen (Di Costanzo, 2000, p. 9). In other words, the island of Ischia has set the foundation, through multi-faceted imagination, its image of being a meeting point or a place for "finding oneself" for those who are looking for areas in which they can find otherness, distance and separation; they are looking for an "elsewhere" to which they can compare themselves…. a different territory, which in the context of the modern world—in many ways a conformist one lacking originality—seems to be disappearing.

"It seems as if time has stopped in Ischia" wrote Truman Capote (Cf., Buchner, 2002, p. VIII). And even King Louis I of Bavaria must have experienced the same feeling, for after having been to Ischia he had someone write on the frescoes of his Royal Garden: "Run to Ischia, away from the hubbub of life, for there you will find the peace that for years has slipped away" (Buchner, 2002, ibid.). The poetics of natural and foreign areas is manifested for some authors as a dreamlike form, but it is a dream come true: "the island is far away from the fast pace of today's men, always yearning for novelties….a pace which seems to calm down before the memory of myths and stories of long ago that emerge from the faces, gestures or language of islanders that one is still lucky enough to encounter….myths and stories that emerge from crumbling ruins, fortresses and defense towers, from the continual emergence of fire and sulfur buried by the land, from the gush of waters that burns yet soothes the evils of men "(Deuringer, 1959, p 10). And it is this dimension of serenity and well-being, requested and found by many travelers on "the green island", that has given this place a magical significance…it is a dimension which is well-formed thanks to the splendour generated by the landscape's diversity. Perhaps it was this wealth of contrasting elements that evoked for Berkley the idea that Ischia is the "epitome of the whole world" (Di Meglio, b1987, p 25).

In addition, the nature, the history, the culture of modernity. Discovered by philosophers, from literature, the island becomes a meeting point of several characters, of different cultural fields. Then the meetings between directors, actors, island pictures, love between artists and territory, have enriched the environment of a surplus value of the image, and this included "imaginary" stirs up new cultural attractions, in an incessant feedback. The world of filmmaking could not remain indifferent to all that. Ischia, both as a filming location for other places, allusive as the stage herself, welcomed a large production of films. Not only has allowed the creation of Epic such as the historic "Cleopatra", but also hosted a lot of small productions and, secondarily, out-and-out pure film cassette. All this has led definitely, even perhaps subliminally, the increase of knowledge from a wide catchment area and a huge as unexpected publicity worldwide. And since the film, for the illusion of reality that characterizes it, exercises on a particular audience suggestion, Ischia becomes inspiring for many filmmakers that end up considering the island an ideal setting. The cinematic interest is, however, not only about the "aesthetics", Ischia is also very circumscribed space and helpfully varied, but also very limited in its extent, to the extent necessary to make long journeys for people and vehicles, resulting in cost savings and profitable production.
Probably also why the island has been scenario of choice for the most disparate: love, adventure, mystery, comedy, drama, historical. As we shall see, the film epic and historical cutting occupy a prominent place in the cinematic history of the island. Maybe it's because Ischia is a place so rich in history and traditions, historical memory. Our journey in the imagination can only Ischia from the

island's history. Far be it from us to develop a complete and comprehensive historical treatment of the subject, which goes beyond the objectives of our work and that would require other tools and research possibilities. Given the nature and purpose of this book, we'll simply to outline some essential clues of life, which seem essential to the development of our route of analysis and reflection.

Besides the nature, the history, and the modern culture, and besides having been discovered by philosophers and literature, the island has become a meeting point of several characters of different cultural fields. Consequently, the meetings between directors, actors, islanders, love between artists and the territory have all enriched the environment of contributions to the island's image; this endowment of 'idealistic traits' creates new cultural interest via incessant feedback. The world of filmmaking could not remain indifferent to all that. Ischia, both as a filming location serving to simulate other places and as a filming location serving as the stage of itself, welcomed a large production of films. Not only has it allowed for the creation of colossal movies such as the historic "Cleopatra" but it also hosted a lot of smaller productions and, not of lesser value, authentic cassette films. All this has definitely led, perhaps even subliminally, to the increase of Ischia's familiarity to a huge audience and to great, unexpected publicity worldwide. Since the cinema world, for the illusion of reality that characterizes it, uses the element of fascination for audiences, Ischia becomes inspiring for many filmmakers that end up considering the island as an ideal setting. The cinematic interest is, however, not only about the "aesthetics"; Ischia is also a very circumscribed space and advantageously varied, but also very limited in its extent, to the point that it is not necessary to have people and vehicles move across long distances, thereby resulting in advantageous production cost savings. Perhaps it is even for this reason that the island has been the chosen setting for the production of a wide variety of films: love, adventure, mystery, comedy, drama, historical. As we shall see, epic and historical movies occupy a prominent place in the cinematic history of the island. Maybe it's because Ischia is a place so rich in history, traditions, and historical memories. Our journey into the imaginary world evoked by Ischia must absolutely start from the island's history. It is not our intention to develop a complete and comprehensive historical description, as this would go beyond the objectives of our work and would well require other tools and research opportunities. Given the nature and purpose of this book, we'll simply outline some essential points of the historical sequence of events of the site which seem fundamental to the development of our journey based on analysis and reflection.

1.2 Pithecusa's Past

An analysis of the many finds discovered reveals that the island must have been inhabited as of the Neolithic times. Traces of human settlement from the Paleolithic era have not been found probably because of volcanic activity. Traces of human settlement reappear but from the Bronze Age, according to evidence found of a village that existed on the Castiglioni hill and to the remains of another settlement in Lacco Ameno (Buchner, Rittmann, 1948, p. 43).
In the fourteenth century BC, the Mycenaeans landed on the island and ran the commercial traffic in the

Mediterranean. In the Iron Age it appears that only the Casamicciola area was inhabited while the rest of the island was abandoned for reasons that are unknown (Di Meglio, A2001, p. 65).

Very clear traces of effective colonization of the island date back to the 8th century BC when the Eritreans of Euboea and the Chalcidians settled, probably looking for new commercial outlets (Ielasi, 1987, p. 8).

The island's first name was *Pithecussai*, to which is ascribed a double meaning: "the island of monkeys" (from *pithechi*, monkeys) –monkeys which, according to myth, "traded places" with the crafty and malicious Cercopi --or "the island of the clay pots" (from *Pathos*, large clay pot), produced by the dedicated work of local communities (Deuringer, 1959, p. 55).

In this period, the island began its (first) economic and civil ascent, becoming a cutting-edge town in which flowed different cultures: Italic, Greek and Eastern. No other Greek site can boast of the discovery of objects from such a wide variety of people: the Corinthian vessels, Syrian seals, Egyptian scarabs, Euboean pottery, Phoenician amphoras, as well as several items imported from various Italian regions and more (Malagoli, 1987, pp 8-9).

It appears that the Greeks themselves "exported" a lot of different and important cultural acquisitions (Cf., Hillman, 2004), an example being of them teaching the people with whom they came into contact the ancient Chalcidian alphabet from which derived Etruscan writing and then Latin. Moreover, epic poetry seems to be no stranger to this context: a cup, "Nestor's cup", found unfortunately in pieces in a cremation grave and later rebuilt in its entirety. There is an inscription on it that refers to the eleventh canto of the Iliad: *"Whoever drinks from this cup will immediately be seized by the desire for the beautifully-crowned Aphrodite."* In fact, the ancient Greeks also imported grapes and olive trees to Pithecusa, resources which in time would become very important for the entire island's economy (Deuringer, 1959, p. 70).

The promontory of Monte Vico, with its peculiar structure with three sides facing the sea, became the acropolis, while the two bays of "Under Varuli" and "San Montano" functioned for a long time as commercial and strategic retreat ports for ships, in case of attacks. These were features that responded fully to the logistical needs of the settled community. Probably as a result of internal conflicts, or because of the volcanic eruption in 750 BC, the Eritreans and the Chalcidians abandoned Pithecusa to found the city of Cuma (Malagoli, 1987, p.10). However, in 474 BC the island was ceded by Cumans to the tyrant Hiero of Syracuse, who realized at various points different artifacts, not only on the area currently occupied by the Aragonese Castle which perhaps was already at that time serving a defensive purpose, receiving a garrison. The term "round", referring to this site, probably derives from the Roman city walls which at the time surrounded the neighboring village and the hilltop (Di Meglio, A2001, p.184). Other researchers believe instead that the origin of the name is to be traced to the expression "Castrum Gironis"; basically, the site welcomed a building erected on a small island, circular in shape, which you could circumnavigate by boat. In fact, it was not until the next phase of the Castle's development that it was connected to the rest of the island by a bridge. In any case, with the advance of Roman power and the decline of the hegemony of Greek politics in Neapolis the Island of Ischia was strongly subjected to Rome's influence. With the victory of Silla, Pithecusa was taken away from Naples so that it could fall under Roman rule. The island was destroyed and the people were deprived of all rights. The name of the island transformed into Aenaria. The Romans built the first thermal baths and in the 700s the remains of the votives for the nymphs of Nitrodi were found--twelve marble reliefs that prove how the fountain bearing the same name was for the people of the Empire was not just a spa facility, but a place of worship as well (Monti, 1968).

In 29 B.C. the Emperor Augustus returned the island to Naples, taking Capri in exchange. With the barbaric invasions that followed, Aenaria fell under Byzantine rule (D'ax, 1864) then Lombard rule, maintaining at times some type of autonomy. Anyway, from 661-1113 Ischia had the opportunity to be led by its own governor bearing the title of Count (Di Meglio, A 2001, p.80).

In 1134 the island lost its independence and became part of the Norman possessions. What followed was the domination of the Swabians and that of French Anjou family, under whose rule, in the fourteenth century, there was the last violent eruption near present-day Fiaiano.

The violent lava slid to the sea, through today's Ischia Porto and Ischia Ponte, thus destroying the urbanized area. In 1414, Alfonso V of Aragon, the first king of Naples (nicknamed "the Magnanimous"), witnessed, to his favor, the end of the historical struggles between the Anjou and the Aragonese. The Aragonese rule coincided, unfortunately, with the mass deportation of the male islanders who had sided with the Angevins, while their women were forced to "unjust weddings" with the new rulers. Like the predecessors, at the beginning of the fifteenth century A.D. the Aragonese settled on the Castle, erected a mighty defense system and encouraged the growth of the city within its walls. To facilitate access to the castle which represented a place of refuge probably already at the time of Hiero, Alfonso of Aragon had a stone bridge built so that the castle was connected to the rest of the island. Thanks to him, the Castle also became an important place of political and cultural initiatives. Women also played a vital role there, such as Lucrezia d'Alagna and poetess Vittoria Colonna, who in 1509 was united in marriage to Francesco Ferrante d'Avalos, Marquis of Vasto and Pescara (D'ax, 1864). The fortress was a meeting place for artists, poets, and thinkers and consequently the particularity of the island echoed in the verses of great writers, such as Jacopo Sannazzaro, Bernardo Tasso, Ludovico Ariosto. Ischia also appears in the prose of Bembo and is also mentioned in the history of Italy by Guicciardini (D'ax, 1864, p.187).

At the end of 1500s, at the request of Beatrice Quadra, the wife of Muzio D'Avalos, a section of the castle was transformed into a monastery for the Clarissa nuns. At the same time, there was a depopulation of the Castle in favour of the site across from it (modern Ischia Ponte) on which there was already a medieval settlement named "Burgo Maris", later to become the Borgo di Celsa for the presence of mulberries. This village welcomed the bishop's headquarters, several homes of the aristocracy and religious buildings (D'ax, 1864, p. 423).

Already as of the second half of the 1400s, the island had to protect itself against the countless pirate attacks from North Africa. In fact, in Forio, in the west side of the island, numerous watchtowers were erected.

After the Spanish vice regal domain (ca 1501-ca 1700), the short Austrian rule (1710 ca-1734ca), the

Bourbon period (ca 1734-ca 1860) - which included the establishment of the French under Napoleon's rule and of the Neapolitan Republic - it was with the final return of the Bourbons that the island was able to experience a degree of calm, and in 1860 was part of the Kingdom of Italy as part of the province of Naples, as is still the case today (D'Ascia, 1864).

From then on, the island acquired its own identity, intensified the flow of visitors and increasingly became the resort coveted by lovers of nature, the sea, the island's people—people who appreciate its particular traits in different ways.

Throughout the 1800s, as we shall see later, the island strengthened its vocation, in the tourist sense, as a travel destination and vacation spot. Of course, today it is more difficult to imagine poets and writers fleeing the city to come to Ischia to enjoy its wildness, its Arcadian feeling, and its rural ambiance. The island still has stretches of beautiful unspoiled nature, yet on other levels the typical characteristics of the city scene are embedded within it.

Yet, in the recent past there have been many showmen and philosophers, artists and aesthetes who found on the island a place of ancient beauty and true serenity. The body of evidence, in this sense, is truly abundant. From the stories of so many writers one "discovers" how their time is spent on the island, what kind of stimuli they have obtained from their stay and what types of relationship they maintained with its inhabitants.

1.2 The Indigenous Look

How have indigenous islanders appeared to visitors? According to the travel memories of many past visitors, the islanders are not always regarded in a positive light; on the contrary, sometimes visitors experienced true "xenophobia". In fact, Berkeley said that "the inhabitants of Forio and Buonopane were violent and irascible" and narrates stories of fights and knives. Stendhal, passing through Ischia in 1834, even judged the islanders as "savages of Africa" (D'Ambra, 1987).

The legendary author of "Red and Black" wrote: "I spend four very pleasant hours with Don Ferdinand, who hates us, and with good inhabitants of the island. They are savages of Africa. They lack knowledge of their dialect. They live depending on their grapevines. There is almost no trace of civilization "(Di Costanzo, 2000, p. 18).

Benedetto Croce, who at the age of 17 years survived the earthquake of Casamicciola of 1883, judged the Casamicciolesi as "People that did not care about anything, not even about earning money ..." (D'Ambra, 1987).

We could go on with the accounts of this type, but will not add more to the noted observations made by travelers—notes revealing that the islanders "did not like these strangers, who pretended to be interested in their lives, for they looked everything and everyone in the very same way"(Di Costanzo, 2000, p. 16).

Of course, compared to the past, the island has today become a completely different area: the huge flow of tourists, to which the islanders have adapted over time, has forced the islanders to deal with different cultures and understand the benefits of this relationship for the economy of the place. In the testimonies of some islanders, especially the older generation, what still remains imprinted and alive in their memory is the arrival of American directors or anyone else who has made a film on the island, especially for profitable opportunities.

It seems, however, that several directors have often complained about the conduct of the islanders who appeared as "profiteers", as people who customarily demanded money for various reasons: for alleged losses for having to remove laundry from the balconies, for elusive rights of way, for compensation for the violation of their privacy, and for many other weird reasons.

1.4 The Island's Location

The island has always welcomed a very interesting set of anthropological elements comprised of: representatives of the great world and simple holidaymakers, characters of the Jet Set and tourists undergoing thermal spa treatments, rich traders, professionals who are more or less either sophisticated or snobby, and simple peasants of the place. But, by abandoning the typical paths taken by tourists, those who want to explore it will always find the old charm of the island and its inhabitants. It takes maybe chatting in several art galleries with some local genius or, better yet, having a conversation with the old fishermen of Ischia Ponte, in the ancient village of Celsa which has not renounced its traditions and preserves almost unchanged the size and the image of typical marine community.

But the ancient atmosphere can also be seen by strolling through the narrow, winding streets of the old part of Forio, or even climbing on foot or on a mule on Mount Epomeo. In the streets of the mountain villages Serrara Fontana and Barano, time in some areas has really stood still. In Panza, grape growers still do their harvesting the old-fashioned way, and it is still possible to encounter women carrying baskets full of grapes over their heads as they did centuries ago. Sant'Angelo, the picturesque fishing village in the far south of the island, a charming treasure of natural landscape and unique architecture, is still, thankfully, barred to cars. All of this in many ways contrasts with the glitz or the "urban" modern atmosphere present in the elegant shops of Via Roma and Corso Vittoria Colonna, between Ischia Porto and Ischia Ponte, the typical restaurants, the noise of the ferries and numerous pubs, disco bars and hangouts. In short, the green island of Ischia will not let itself be limited in definition by having a precise label as its identity, for it is impossible to confer onto it an unambiguous definition: it is a complex network of many cultural trajectories, so many images, so many ways of being. As for the film industry, many directors have chosen to take a greater interest in some sites rather than in others, even as they built those holographic clichés, those postcard-like images with which Ischia is known worldwide and on which one usually focuses collective attention. The impressive Aragonese Castle, the ancient castle island of great historical value, harmoniously integrated with the landscape, becomes a symbol of battles, adventures, love stories, myths and legends which took place in different eras, as was the case with the filming of "Cleopatra". The fortress, located on the highest point of the Castle--which in 1823 was the site for life imprisonment of criminals and which was later used as a place of punishment for political prisoners—also became an impenetrable prison where "Dr. Antonio" was imprisoned, a protagonist of the eponymous patriotic film which told the story of a revolutionary who was captured and imprisoned for his participation in the riots of 1848.

Of no less importance is the sixteenth-century "Chiesa del Soccorso", symbol of the town of Forio.

and one of the most unique architectural finds of the island. It is a favorite place for many directors who have tried to catch in their films, at sunset, the extraordinary "green ray"--one of the most attractive "dusk sky shows" that nature can offer. The church is the backdrop, repeatedly recognizable, of films like "Hammer Bells", in which the church represents an orphanage, or "What happened between my father and your mother", where it represents a morgue.

Another location used repeatedly in films is the picturesque village of Sant'Angelo, an exquisite site of Mediterranean colors, of houses huddled together, and of ancient streets that are full of life until late at night by the laughter of the tourists and the live music of various taverns. Not far from the village, the beautiful promontory of S. Angelo, jutting out from the sea, is well recognized in the film "Fox Hunting", but also in the famous "Purple Noon".

Another characteristic symbol of the island is the Lacco Ameno Mushroom (an ancient mass of tufa stone) called by the ancients "the rock of red mullet". It has appeared several times in Cineriz films, from "Holiday in Ischia" to "Operation Ischia Love" to "Appointment in Ischia "and can be counted among the most famous icons of the island on a global scale. What eventually became a privileged location, particularly for these films (all produced by Rizzoli) is the property of the REGINA ISABELLA hotel with its attached baths.

CHAPTER II: The Age of the First Movie Theatre. The Island during the Period of Italian Unification.

2.1 "Cinema Unione": The Dreams of the Ischitans.

In a social and economic context that was quite lacking in cultural events, similar to the one characterizing the island at the beginning of the 1900s, fertile ground is found by the first investors in the field of film screenings. In the dark halls of cinemas, on their big screens, collective dreams seem to settle and stratify, perilous adventures come to life and tough projects, passions and desires come alive. As is well remembered by the spectators, the plots of the films were often interwoven with their own experiences and so, even if in the late nineteenth and early twentieth century the economy was not at all flourishing in Ischia, the first cinema was born: the "Cinema Unione."

A journey of consumption and film production followed a complex strategy—within the island's character-- which linked in various ways the needs of "free time", material needs, the desires of "evasion", and economic needs. In this sense, it is now necessary to develop some thoughts on certain essential aspects of the socio-economic dimension of the territory of Ischia of that period.

2.2 The Problem of Monoculture: the Ischitan Vine Variety

In which social context was the first movie theater born and how did the desire and the importance of going to the movies come to be?

Ischia, a long-standing tourism destination for its thermal spas, popular in this capacity since the 16th century, was, however, the privilege of only a few and the flow of visitors never developed equally across the entire island. The tourism industry was mainly family-run and concerned the middle class, especially Neapolitans. Tourists stayed in the few boarding houses available and vacationers rented houses, thereby contributing modest wealth to the general economy of the island. The tourism was eventually greatly reduced because of the catastrophic earthquakes of 1881 and 1883 which destroyed the spa town of Casamicciola Terme, compromising the future work of both the operators engaged in this sector, as well as those who were connected to the sector indirectly (such as those who were dedicated to working with clay in order to manufacture "riggiole" (*tiles*) and tools). These individuals had to turn to certainly less profitable jobs such as the processing of straw.

Poverty in this period was so obvious that the farmers did their best to use any source in order to improve production. They gathered both animal manure and human organic debris—which, given the poor sanitation of the time, were "deposited" in the streets—and mixed it with the dry seaweed that the sea rejected ashore. The compound that was obtained was used as fertilizer, especially in swampy areas, to make the land cultivable.

But how and why it did such a burdensome situation arise? The reasons are different, but at this point we will try to analyze some of them, at least those that seem most important.

Agriculture, a key resource for the island, was not a productive enough industry, certainly not enough to satisfy the needs of the islanders. On the one hand, this was due to the unreliability of the soil quality, and secondly it was due to the fact that at the time the land available was used almost exclusively for the cultivation of vines--but an economy based on a single product is always weak.

Added to this situation was the occurrence of land fragmentation, resulting from the abolition of the rights of primogeniture, as well as other forms of peasant impoverishment (Cf., Arias, 1921) caused by 'ecclesiastical mortmain'. Anyway, between the late eighteenth and early nineteenth centuries, there were the first divisions of properties which then continued as an unstoppable process. The continued division of funds resulting from small and very small properties made the landowner income increasingly inadequate for the lives of families who owned broken up pieces of land. These pieces of land were often situated with considerable distances between them, as situation which made it even more difficult to have them managed which of course led to scarce production. (Di Meglio A,2001).

The situation worsened further when the first phylloxera infestation manifested itself.

The Ischitan economy, which was based mainly on the wine trade, ended up being threatened for a long period of time. A solution came only towards the first half of the 19th century, when some grape fungicide sprayers, the San Filippo brothers, came from Lipari and applied copper sulfate on the grape vines for the first time in Ischia (Mancini, 1980).

2.3 Customs and Traditions: The 'Carusiello' Ballad

The overall conditions of the construction industry's assets were very precarious, as were those of the residential construction jobs. In the 1930s, although the town encouraged construction, this was not easily achievable due to the shortage of materials. Tuff, not directly available on the island, was imported from Pozzuoli, and lime had to be kneaded by hand, something the islanders had great difficulty in doing, especially since machinery was practically non-existent. In other words, construction jobs had to almost be done completely by hand, thereby greatly reducing the technical performance and economic yield. Then there was a chronic shortage of fresh water which was accompanied by high labor costs, the lack of an adequate network of internal roads and substantial ignorance about the configuration of zoning.

Perhaps, partly as a result of these "constraints", the technique to build a house (Cf., Truppi, 1991; 1999), which was always under the influence of different environmental compatibilities, --social and economic-- had remained almost unchanged on the island until the 1960s. The rooms were made up of solid supporting perimeter walls that supported a vaulted system, the whole process ending off with the beating of the paving by doing a rhythmic dance "to *'vattut' e ll'astec"* (the beating of the paving) which turned into a ritual dance for this final part of the construction process. This dance represented the job of covering the roofs with a characteristic dome called "carusiello", a name recalling in some way the Arab architecture (Sardella, 1985).

Early in the morning, after preparing the mixture of lapillus and lime the house owner would tie a flag to a long chestnut pole to make it visible in the distance. It was the signal announcing this roof making event, rallying young robust men in the district because to collaborate in the project for free. It was a party: the peasants would pin down their hoes and abandoned fields as they flocked to contribute their arm power—arms that were accustomed to hard work. At dawn came the batsmen or "puntanari" would also arrive with their own sticks, and with rhythmic and violent blows they would continually splash the lapilli with lime stucco. It was hard work to incessantly move around and around the dome; (Cacciapuoti, 1961) the various movements characterizing the work would be emphasized by the sounds of clarinets and drums. Everyone would be taken in by the vortex of a frenzied dance, the conclusion of which coincided with the end of this reunion of workers.

The workers, in this way, proudly proved their skills and strength. A short break would be taken to eat a donut and guzzle some wine, then one would get back to work. In the evening everyone would gather at the table. To regain one's strength from the exhausting labors, one would enjoy a meal of rabbit, donuts and wine voraciously. A Bacchus-style ritual, a real rejoicing consisting of jokes, songs and dances. Even today, the folk group of Buonopane "A 'ndrezzata" (Deuringer, 1959) repeats the ritual of dome making accompanied by music at an ever-increasing rate which hypnotizes the audience and involves them emotionally. Maybe it is precisely for these moments of social gathering, the celebrations dedicated to almost any event, that the Green Island still retains the idea, in the imagination of its visitors, that "in Ischia you eat, drink and whistle ".

2.4 "Merecoppe": Memories of Everyday Life

In the country rich area known as "Merecoppe", located at the southern side of the island, the inhabitants' living conditions were in some ways better than those of the other inhabitants of the island: they ate the products of their fields, the food produced by their animals (i.e. eggs), and the animals they raised on their farms. Ms. Angela, entrusting her account to telecommunications like a message in a bottle, described in a very effective manner the way of life in the country, evoking memories of her family who had lived in the early 1900s. We report here excerpts of her story.

"Buonopane, was a country of farmers; grapes were grown, legumes were sowed and on the high ground wheat was sown. Once the wheat matured, it was placed on the roofs and knocked down and deprived of straw, thanks to the wind. In "nasselle" (*small boats*) white and black figs were set out to dry out so as to be consumed later in the winter.

At one time the carriages used by foreigners used to be stationed where the buses are today; the horses were fed with grass that "merecuppesi" (so were called the people of "merecoppe" in the local jargon), would sell. Already at three in the morning, although the temperatures were hot, the women walked toward the port, carrying large baskets on their heads filled with fruits of the land; with the sale's proceeds they bought fish and offal for lunch and for dinner.

In addition to working at home, they helped the men in the fields and in autumn would go into the woods to collect dry leaves of chestnut trees to make "beds" for the pigs. Once such beds would be soiled, they would be used as fertilizer.

Although every house had a cistern to collect rain water, in the summer the girls went to stock up on the precious liquid from the Nitrodi fountain.

In every home there was a hearth with an oven for baking bread. There was also almost always a washboard to wash clothes, sheets, fabrics in general, and much more, a procedure called "a culata" in jargon. It was a process that lasted three days and required, in addition to soap, baked ash.

The homes had only a few, essential furnishings and

there were large beds where four or five people would sleep together.

The bathrooms were poor: nothing but a hut made of branches. Subsequently, they were replaced by "Turkish bathrooms"; once in a while, when the tanks of such bathrooms were cleaned, the sewage that had accumulated there was used to fertilize the fields. Men worked the land, but sometimes they would have fun too! When it was raining or too cold, for example, they would get together with friends in a cellar and for this occasion would roast dried beans or some smoked fish, all accompanied by new wine. At the end of the evening, they returned home a little tipsy.

At that time there was great harmony between family members, so in the countryside everyone ate all together from a large bowl; if there was no fork, you could eat with a reed, and if there was no spoon, an onion layer was attached to the fork or to the reed.

The only family income came from wine sales and each family had a goat to always have milk available and to produce excellent cheeses. In the village there was only one flock that the shepherd would lead to the streets every morning to sell milk. They also bred pigs and consumed every part of them, including the blood which would be collected in containers to make the so-called "sanguinaccio" (a black pudding), a typical sweet.

The farmers prepared for the grape harvest a week before by organizing the wine cellar and preparing the tools that were used for the event: the barrels were washed, the press was cleaned, and the concrete basins were wiped and disinfected with boiling water. The bunches of grapes were cut with curved knives, scissors or dropped in the "tinelli", vessels of fitted wood staves while table grapes (of the type known as "regina" or "pane") were collected in the

" cufanella ", a basket without a handle, for family consumption. After the grapes were gathered and placed into a big, concrete basin, barefoot would go into the basin and crush the grapes while singing songs.

Even for children, the grape harvest was a time of joy and unity, but some of them remember with little pleasure the obligation to collect the grapes from the ground so that not one grape would go to waste.

At about ten in the morning large mixed salads were prepared. One tasty salad was the "fusciata" made with: stale bread soaked in water and wrung out, leaves of "paprastiello" (a type of lettuce), tomatoes, radishes, oil, salt and wine. Before eating this, the entire salad would soak in vinegar for two days, thereby being dressed with wine. Other times, with the addition of other ingredients one created the "caponata", which is eaten even today.

Each event was a reason to get together as a family. On the last evening of the harvest, there would be a big family feast (the "scialattiello") at which one would eat pasta which was obtained from the ground wheat, rabbit, salad, meat and sometimes salami.

Most of the boys, now grandparents, did not have toys and used with their mothers' pots and brooms. The girls would make some rag doll or a doll made of wool, while the boys were playing with little wheeled vehicles, that is, wooden carts. They enjoyed themselves outdoors. A board game was the famous "Campana" that we still know today.

2.5 Lacco Ameno: Fishing and Crafts

Before the economic boom, the inhabitants of Lacco Ameno lived essentially off of the income generated from modest farming or fishery, or gains from the "tonnara" (a fishing system for catching tuna), one of the last fishing systems that has endured in the Gulf of Naples.

The "tonnara" of Lacco Ameno, with the dense nets that composed it, its two large boats, the "scicc" and "caparrais" and their respective crews, undertook a number of employees who would work now and then mainly for poor earnings. The docking of the large boats, caulking holes on the hull and the subsequent departure from the port helped time pass quickly while fishing. The other resource that supplied the island territory was agriculture, while for some, to make ends meet, they would try to produce whatever they could with straw (Mennella, 1999, p. 16).

Straw or *erba carosella*, was produced in Serrara Fontana, the area from which keen women, barefoot or with clogs, would travel long distances to other locations on the island in order to sell or trade the "precious" straw good. These straw products were not only produced by women, but also by men when they were free from other work and the kids….the men worked on the less tedious stages of the fabrication process. In time the people have, in some ways become better equipped to improve the processing and marketing of straw products. In fact, today there are many who devote themselves to manufacturing straw hats, bags, baskets and fans, all greatly appreciated by tourists….but as we know, the tradition goes way back in time. (Mennella, 1999, p. 15).

2.6 The Terracotta Fishermen

Among the typical activities that were "historically" part of the island's economy and survived to the present day, we certainly cannot forget the tradition of terracotta production which has remained more or less unchanged since the time of the Greeks to the present day; one must note, however, that over time it has lost its productive value based on "daily needs" to acquire less "industrial" character and increasingly more artistic character. For centuries these artifacts were to serve the most diverse technical requirements such as creating floors, bricks, pipes, various tools and more. Today the glorious tradition of Ischia ceramics, present a bit all over the island, has extended to create refined objects for tourists. Few are the artisans who, mainly upon request, still produce items from the ancient tradition of Ischia necessary for carrying out various restoration operations.

Peculiar is the bond of fishing with terracotta. A system to catch the octopus was in fact to use the amphorae, the so-called "Lancelle". This technique, which has remained unchanged for centuries and continued up to the 70s, is today distinguished by the use of iron boxes, while "Lancelle" are used today as a mere embellishment for the homes, such as ornaments and much more. A great innovative factor for the fishing industry's production, but especially for the living and working conditions of the islanders, was the advent of the internal combustion engine. The "ambulance" (if what we are about to describe can be called as such) which is basically the means of transportation for the sick, was at the time a fishing boat with 4 oars with a straw mattress on the boat's cauldron on which they placed the sick person while carrying him/her to promontory closest to the island: Torre Gaveta in Pozzuoli. One can imagine the practicality and the inconvenience of this system when the sea was rough.

Fishing, not one of the leading businesses for the island's economy, a reality shared also by the other islands of the south, was carried out until the beginning of the 1900s with fishing lines, or rather, with horsehair and fish traps made of woven straw whose production involved the whole family. How could anyone with such equipment revive an economy? A major change came with the appearance of nylon, but fishing remained relegated to a marginal economic sphere, so much so that with respect to the catch, the practice of bartering was still used, a practice that could be understood in a broad sense as an "exchange."

In Ischia the phenomenon of "CALA - CALA" was characteristic (Algranati, 1959, pp 85-94).

The fisherman would go under some cliff that would have villages or homes over it, and screaming these words he called the peasants, for example the inhabitants of the mountainous area of San Pancrazio, who would drop a basket containing vegetables and whatever else they had produced, in exchange for fish products. In Forio, however, strangely with these words a very different phenomenon would be indicated: someone stealing from other people's fruit trees.

It is interesting to note that even within a small area like that of an island, different cultures and traditions have been established and consequently the same expressions can have different meanings in relation to situations that affect the daily life.

Tourism, which was not developed in the same manner across the island, was mainly a family-run industry, the island was a quiet destination for vacationers mainly belonging to the middle Neapolitan bourgeoisie. At that time there were few room and boards, so for the entire summer season the islanders rented even their own homes to vacationers while making do as best as possible in smaller houses. In any case, the resources generated from the rents provided the tenants with a modest and in some cases even discrete affluence which was reflected in the general economy of the island.

2.7 The Opening of the Theatres: The Islanders Go to the Movies

In this socio-economic context of 1936, the first time arrival in Ischia of film crews to shoot the film "The Black Corsair" (and the next year the filming of " Dr. Antonio ") caused a notable change in the island's situation of widespread insecurity, thereby triggering a certain economic dynamism which subsequently enabled a slow but steady transformation of the island's productive and social fabric.

This overview of the "memory" of the contextualized island is intended to show the social and anthropological basis on which the mechanism of development was linked to cinematographic art, even from the point of view of the initiative taken by the first entrepreneurs who understood the importance of film and therefore of the places in which suitable spaces suitable for the projections for large audiences could be equipped. Already at the end of the 1920s the first three move theatres appear on the island. As they were frequented, they revealed how the islanders immediately considered the theatres as important places for social gatherings, fun, but also a means through which one could escape from the narrow confines of a "restricted" world, from a very limited reality. Movie theatres were also seen as a tool serving to unleash one's imagination and to dream of a different, fantastic dreamlike world which replaces the known "hard" reality for a few hours and sublimates the idealism of a difficult existential condition.

The first license issued for the opening of a movie theater was assigned to Luigi Castagna in the summer of 1929. The theatre was that of "CINEMA

UNIONE", commonly known like all the other theatres of the province as 'Pidocchietto' ("louse", a nickname that revealed that there was usually a high likelihood of leaving the theatres in the company of unwelcome guests). The first screenings of this cinema were aimed at featuring silent films and works of theatrical inspiration. The second license was obtained by Catello Gloria on January 12, 1930 for the "CINEMA CONTE"; this licence was then passed to Antonio Pascariello on May 27, 1931. The third license was granted to Restituta Anastasio for the " CINEMA EXCELSIOR ". It was officially inaugurated in 1956 with the screening of the movie "Anastasia", starring Ingrid Bergman (Cf., Mancusi, 1989).

Subsequently, within a few years in various municipalities islanders were witnessing the opening of the "CINEMA AURORA" in Barano, the "CINEMA MODENA" in Forio (known today as "CINEMA DELLE VITTORIE"), the "CINEMA ITALIA" in Casamicciola and "CINEMA REGINELLA" in Lacco Ameno.

As of 1956 onward, however, with the spread of television there was reversal in movie interest, as was the case in other parts of Italy (other types of consumer goods increased thereby causing setbacks for cinematographic demands). Even in Ischia many theatres were forced to close before reaching the current situation in which only the "CINEMA EXCELSIOR " in the municipality of Ischia and the "CINEMA DELLE VITTORIE" in the municipality of Forio are still in operation. In any case, the story of the movie theatres in Ischia is a matter of great interest as it overlaps with the complex sequence of events of the transformations that accompanied the evolution of the overall character of the island and its progressive goals. To tell this entire story is virtually impossible, but some evidence that we have collected is very useful to reconstruct the climate, the atmosphere, and the enthusiasm and hopes of that era. Luigi Cesareo is the grandson of Luigi Castagna who was the true pioneer of entrepreneurship involved in the film industry on the island. Here are the highlights of his account.

"Filmmaking, as is known, sprouted at the end of the nineteenth century. A few years after its invention, my maternal grandfather had the idea of creating a cinema on the island of Ischia, so he rented a piece of the garden belonging to the former Augustinian monastery. It was a place of rich, cultural memories; it even housed a drawing a Giacinto Gigante. It was in this way that he created the first Ischitan theatre: it was in a shed of about 150 square meters. Over the years, the movie screenings followed the various stages of Italian cinematography: first, silent movies, then the sound films, finally the advent of color films. In the 1920s and 1930s, in addition to movies release the theatres also hosted theatrical performances. Initially, during the screenings of silent films, the images were accompanied by live played soundtracks. Maestro Francesco Iacono, a pianist nicknamed the young Marquis, was responsible for this music. The name "CINEMA UNIONE" is derived, of course, from the historical period in which it was built; in other words, it was dedicated to the unification of Italy which had occurred shortly after the theatre's construction. In Campania – he remembers - in the early years of the last century there were a few cinemas, located between Naples, Ischia and a few other locations. My grandfather Luigi Castagna died in 1954, leaving behind nine children. In 1960 he was also honored for his 50 years of entrepreneurial activity with a gold medal by the president of the Republic, Segni, who brought it to the presidential palace to stay. During the summer of the 1920s and 1930s, it was he who invented on the island "outdoor film screenings" by using some beautiful beaches of Ischia's shores. After the war, other movie theatres emerged and were engaged in the projection of many Italian and American feature films of that time period. But in the 1930s, the "pizza" films lasted 20 minutes each. They were often put together, then sometimes they were broken up and put back together some way. I have to confess a family secret. Before my grandfather returned each screened movie to the distributor, he cut off a pretty large piece and kept it. After having gathered a good number of pieces, he reassembled these clips at random, of course, thereby creating a weird mix of sequences. When bad weather prevented ships from setting out from Naples, the movies did not come either, so my grandfather introduced the public to the projection of these strange sequences. I officially lay claim to the fact that my grandfather, Luigi Castagna, was the true inventor of Blob. It must be said that when the end of the screening, many viewers who obviously did not understand anything about the film went to complain to my grandfather and asked him for explanations. He replied that they had not understood the plot and the meaning of the film because they had not gone to school and that they were therefore highly ignorant people.

Traditionally on Christmas Eve the most popular films were the antics of Charlie Chaplin and Stanley and Hardy. The people dined very early so that they wouldn't be late for the evening screenings. In the 1950s a ticket costed 150 lire. Usually the movie viewers filled the monastery. The first of the famous long movies of that era, Quo Vadis, La tunica *'The*

Robe', Catene *'Chains'*, Figli di nessuno *'Sons of no one'*, and the videocassette movies with Amedeo Nazzari films, would always have a full house. During that time, especially in the era of the silent movies, movies were in high attendance and viewers watched movies as if they were witnessing real events. It was not uncommon to see people denounce what was bad, and sometimes even criticize the pianist if he did not use music that they thought was suitable. In short, the movie theatre was a place of social and community life; many regular viewers had even established their seats. Up to 1938, the fixed-Christmas appointment was with the movie LA CANTATA DEI PASTORI *'THE SONG OF THE SHEPHERDS'*, whereas at Easter one could not miss the play MORTE E PASSIONE DI CRISTO *'DEATH AND PASSION OF CHRIST'*.

After the war, my grandfather built on a plot located near the street known as Vittoria Colonna the 'GIARDINO D'ITALIA' *"GARDEN OF ITALY"* that existed up to the 1970s. In this place, a well-equipped vast zone, the space was dedicated to various businesses of interest to tourists. In the 1950s there were the bars "La Briciola","Bar Vittoria" and "Monkey". Nightlife in Ischia began there. I remember that when I was a child, the place was frequented by Totò and many other famous movie stars and showmen. Before, the nightlife was mainly concentrated in Piazza Croce, at the Bar Vittoria where the trial court was also located. It is in this way that the development of the tourist area started in the 1950s. Where there is now the Hotel Alexander there was a sleep-away marine camp for boys that also had an ice rink. Its manager, a Neapolitan businessman, also built in the 1950s an arena that was named "La Pineta". In the summer there were two bars on the main street: IL GIARDINO D'ITALIA *'THE*

GARDEN OF ITALY' and the arena LA PINETA *'THE PINE FOREST'*. Television, meanwhile, came into Italian homes. At first only a few had it, then even in Ischia everybody owned one. The economic crisis of movie theatres and more had started. The first facility to close its doors was IL GIARDINO D'ITALIA, in the 1970s. Then came the turn of the historic theatre UNIONE in the early 80s. In the same period the PINETA shut down, then, in the 90s, even the EXCELSIOR theatre closed down.

The situation of the EXCELSIOR was different: it had 800 seats and the screening schedule followed the Italian and international movie trends. In the 20s the UNIONE closed in June, and its equipment was transferred to either the GIARDINO D'ITALIA or LA PINETA. In the summer, the screening schedule indulged the demands of the tourists. Screenings began at about 6 p.m. with a show for children, and ended with a screening at 9 p.m. and even with a night screening that started after midnight. The selection of films for screening was always based on the tastes of the public. For example, horror movies were avoided because the families of the audience did not like them. The elderly Castagna was attentive to technological innovations: with the invention of the cinemascope he had to restructure the environment to make it compatible.

The EXCELSIOR was managed from 1973 to 1989 with a license assigned to the family. The theatre UNIONE also served as the set for the film DELITTO IN PIENO SOLE, *PURPLE NOON*; many scenes were shot inside the building, which actually was not at all suitable. But the logistical problems were solved with quick wit and initiative.

At the time, when a movie was shot, in order to see how the movie turned out the director had to wait for the film strips to be developed in Naples (Ischia didn't have a laboratory). So every day directors previewed the film sequences of the previous day that had arrived from Naples by ferry. Most films shot in Ischia were realized in this fashion. The exception was CLEOPATRA because at the Excelsior a real development laboratory was installed. Today, with the current technology available, thanks to electronics there is no longer the need for the development of images. Everything can be seen in real time, like on television. Yes, television. The true crisis of the cinema UNIONE was when the television program LASCIA O RADDOPPIA began on Thursday evenings. This resulted in a total drop in the number of spectators. Serving as a "quick fix" for the crisis, the theatres set up TVs to allow the public to follow the programs. This was a desperate attempt at keeping customers. But it was all in vain. A few years later everyone had their own TV in the living room. It was the end of an era.

CHAPTER III: Crews arrive on the Island. Directors and actors come to Ischia

3.1 Dreams of Motion-Picture Films

The cinema, since its inception, has proved to be one of the most formidable instruments among the many devices that have structured the imaginary world of modern times (see Abruzzese, 1973). It is a versatile and complex machine able to narrate but also to build "stories" that are capable of uniting reality and dreams, rationality and magic. The world of cinema reveals itself as a mechanism having a deep connection to the evolutionary dimension of the human species because it brings into play elements that relate the most intimate, profound and contradictory aspects of the human being who is, according to Morin "*faber,* maker of tools, *sapiens*, rational and realist, and even together *demens*, manufacturer of ghosts, myths, ideologies "(Morin, 1982, p.10). The film industry thus becomes the basis of negotiations, the product of a dialectic in which one sees the contrast and convergence of the "objective" truth of the image and the "subjective" participation of the viewer. For some scholars, the secret of the film dimension seems to be that of "injecting" into the unreality of the image the reality of movement and of pushing the fictitious world towards a goal that was never reached until its invention (Metz, 1972, p. 45); for others, the film industry teaches us to see what we often are no longer able to perceive in everyday life or that rather we have never really seen (Balaz, 1987).
For many, the movie industry was considered a form of knowledge concerning the structure and the state of society, a code that interprets the social changes,

but also an ideology, an art form. Yet, it is an organized grouping of activities and roles - actors and writers of dialogues, scriptwriters, directors, technicians, actors, distributors - that make up a complex machine, that is, a powerful mass media able to influence public opinion, collective behavior, taste, customs, certain aspects of morality. It is clear that movies "capture" the audience by means of the actors, and "project" in the most diverse stories and without a definite time frame emotions, desires, passions, and dilemmas that belong to everyone and are re-experienced by everyone every time such stories are seen on screen (See Aristarchus, 1984). Moreover, if the film industry is compared to other cultural sources, such as literature and newspapers, one notes that it also has a greater "ability to penetrate inter-class collaboration" which eliminates, for its syncretism, different "distances" that are not only space-time related, unifying places and different people while in investing in the public's curiosity for the "performances" of collective and individual character. Probably, for those who were like the islanders of the past in not having the ability to move about easily, the cinema offered the cheapest ticket for traveling, not only towards the "knowledge" of the geographical and human world, but also to explore, in some manner, their inner world. Indeed, perhaps, in the era of the dawn of cinema, for the people of Ischia the big screen was mainly used to stimulate curiosity and interests of existential, and psychological nature even before those of social nature. On the other hand, live action footage of social phenomena is almost impossible and reality produced by the film industry is always, inevitably, a "reconstructed reality"; and this is in spite of the considerable sociological wherewithal of the film industry which, as can be appreciated in an ethno-anthropological document, is able to describe both the movement and the sequence of actions, lending itself to effectively take into account the social reality (Mattioli, 1991). In fact, it is the film editing that allows for the transformation of reality, reassembling in a coherent or arbitrary, fanciful fashion, the "pieces" of the territory which may become the segments of an infinite imaginary puzzle. For over more than a century, Ischia has been suitable for being used and transformed in various dimensions as a changing scenario of dreams of motion-film pictures, as a workshop for manufacturing the contemporary myth.

3.2 The neorealist island

It seems that even the films produced in Ischia during the period of neo-realism wanted to communicate and interact in many ways with the public in order to establish new relationships between the individual and the community. This genre asserted itself in Italy and Europe after World War II by interpreting, reliably and sincerely, the historical period and by taking a critical look at current events or making links between cinema and society (Brunetta, 1998). The main issues covered included the reconstruction of the country and the denunciation of serious social problems to which there will hopefully be an adequate solution. The camera offers a new model of "reading" film by maintaining the tendency to respect reality by using both the true images and their true deep meanings. In this manner certain techniques of the classic assembly were avoided and as well as spectacular interventions of some "falsifying" mode (Canova, 2002). The camera allows, in this sense, what Malinowski calls the vital contact with reality or synchronism lived, causing the film to become a means of cutting-edge and act as a factor of change. The environments, more or less "natural" choices from time to time, are the cities, the countryside, the suburbs, the streets of poor neighborhoods. The stories tell of hunger, unemployment, backwardness, illiteracy (Brunetta, 1998). In this context, the South, including the island of Ischia, become a special setting.

Although belonging to a dramatic genre, different from neo-realism for its structural and narrative purposes, traces of it as a precursor are found in the film "**Dottor Antonio**", filmed in Ischia in 1937, directed by Enrico Guazzoni, set in the time of the Risorgimento during the riots of 1848. The film tells the story of a southern young doctor who falls in love with an English girl but is forced to leave to go to Naples and take part in the revolution. Unfortunately, he was arrested and sentenced to many years in prison. The patriot is imprisoned in the fortress of the Castello Aragonese but his beloved becomes aware of the place of his detention, corrupts the guards and facilitates his escape.

1949 is the year of production of the film **"L'acqua li portò via"** (*"The water carried them away"*). The work was carried out with a considerable waste of resources but, after being brought to term, was never presented to the public "because the producers went to court to resolve their differences over the film's financing and related gains," at least this is the opinion of the director Rate Furlan (See Chiti Poppi, 1991).

For this film they were used a large number of island extras: among these was Ms. Lina Chizzi Scala, from whom we were able to obtain a commentary. "The film was made in Forio, it did not occur to me now the name of the director, but I remember perfectly the main protagonist: the actress Tecla Scarano. It was a drama, which was an ugly story of prostitutes. However the star did a splendid performance, that's why it won the "silver Ribbon" award for the movie "Matrimonio all'italiana" ("*Marriage Italian style*"), a great success for the protagonists Sophia Loren and Marcello Mastroianni ". Anyway, for the production of "The water carried them away" there were significant financial difficulties and the film was never released in Italian cinemas, although there it appears recorded in the historical archives of Cinecittà.

"I was selected - continues Lina - to play the role of a prostitute… I remember that me and other girls were in a large hall of a brothel, waiting for customers to call on us".

Another interesting film on which there is not, unfortunately, much useful information is the film **"La regina dei Turchi"** (*"The Queen of the Turks"*). It is still the elderly woman Lina who remembers when she was hired to work on it and how she was chosen: "As I walked down the street I heard '*It is her… it's her !!! we found her'*. "I was invited to go to the Regina Palace where the Queen asked me if I wanted to be a part of the movie with the role of queen. I said yes, because at that time with small parts one earned good money. I remember that in the movie I was on a stretcher carried by soldiers, I had a cigarette in one hand and a fan in the other. At one point it was shouted "The Turks... Turks ..." and everyone ran away, while I, the queen, I think I was kidnapped. I would be very pleased to see the movie again. "

In 1949 the movie directed by Francesco de Robertis and produced in Ischia, "**Il Mulatto**", addressed delicate issues such as violence against women, racial differences, harbingers after the war and the major upheavals of social equilibrium. The subjects of the film are, in fact, those who were emphasized in the song "Tammurriata nera." In addition, it is the desired alternation in the film between Neapolitan songs and American music, blues and jazz that reveals a lack of communication between these very different worlds which only had in common, according to the claims made in the film, the trait of marginalization. The protagonist is a mulatto child, born as a result of rape by a black American soldier on a local married girl who died giving birth to the child. The little orphan, desperately trying to be accepted by the widower of the woman, was finally starting to be accepted by him.....until the unexpected arrival of the American child's uncle makes the widower aware that for the sake of the young child, because of the skin color , his place is not in Italy, but in America.

Riccardo D'Ambra, owner of the famous tavern of the island, "Il Focolare", and big fan of the movies filmed on the island, so much so that keeps the most famous posters clearly visible on the walls of his tavern, he has some things to tell. His passion appears to have been born not after being an extra in many of this island's films, but also for the evolution of the island's economy which he attributes to the film industry that set it in motion. He particularly recalls of the movie "Il Mulatto" that the setting of the poster was the office of Vincenzo Colucci and the girl in it 16-year-old Letizia Moauro, daughter of Colonel Moauro, who later became the wife of the set designer Ken Adams. The mother of D'Ambra and the young actress often went for walks together, and because of the friendship between the two, the Moauro was also her godmother. The encounter with Ken Adams appears to have occurred when the designer was taken to the island for the production of the film "Il corsaro dell'isola verde" *("The Green island Corsair")*. Sparks suddenly flew, the two fell in love and were married in Florida. Ken Adams subsequently even obtained an honorary citizenship. Along the lines of this alleged incompatibility between different cultures is also considered the film **"Campane a Martello"** *("Hammer Bells")* (1949) directed by Luigi Zampa and starring Gina Lollobrigida and Eduardo De Filippo.

The social dimension represented in the film is very similar to the daily reality of the islanders immediately after the war. People harshly tried by violence and immense hardship tried in every way to forget the past and start living normally.

Distinctive are the scenes in which the barrels are cleaned after having been neglected for too long; in other words, the scenes in which many undertake the tasks related to winemaking, a very important aspect of the island's economy. There are also sequences in the movie of games, images of people trying to have fun by running in cloth sacks on the beach, even though this occurs against the backdrop of the coast whose scenery looks devastated by bombs. Many houses are reduced to rubble, as appearing in long shots and tracking shots of the foreground. Among these "memories" of violence, one main memory is that of the violence exerted on women's bodies. The painful memory of the many rapes by soldiers of the allied troops and their legacy of children with only one parent. Fatherless and "half-black". In the movie the abandoned children are accommodated in an orphanage, set up in the church of Soccorso, in which the person in charge is a priest, played by Eduardo de Filippo. The pastor tries to fulfill his mission by helping them against the indifference of the country, using every possible means to support them and feed them. This even included the money of a young prostitute who sent him her savings so that he could keep them. Upon the woman's return to the island after having receiving a "travel warrant", she discovers how the priest made use of dirty money.

In 1950, the director Roberto Bianchi Montero filmed "**La scogliera del peccato**" ("*The cliff of sin*"), starring Gino Cervi. The film was made mostly in the town of Forio and tells the story of a woman whose dissolute behavior wreaks havoc in a small seaside village. In other words, she is a "Boccadirosa" (a woman of beautiful lips) ahead of her time that threatens the peace and harmony of an anthropological island that sees the disintegration of familial harmony and the spread of debauchery that leads to the ruin of the whole town (see Mereghetti, 2002). With the death of the "sinner" stability is restored --as in the most classic styled soap operas-- in the community microcosm that fully expresses the traits of what Elias Canetti (1990) would have called "la provincia dell'uomo" ("*Man's province*"). We are, in fact, still in its vicinity with the movie **Città canora** ("*The city of songs*"), produced in 1952 and directed by Mario Costa. The film, partly filmed on the island, is a melodrama that is about the usual misunderstandings between lovers. Added to this are the hidden dangers associated with money. Maria's father, even though he knows that his daughter is in love with the young James, wants her to marry the wealthy Renato. Another interesting film work in the context of the dramatic genre is "**Suor Letizia**" ("*Sister Joy*") or "**Il più grande amore**" ("*The greatest love*") (1957). The film was produced by Angelo Rizzoli, one of the major creators of Ischia's enhanced image and the promoters of important projects concerning the revival and development of the island, in particular in the municipality of Lacco

Ameno. The movie producer collaborated with the film's director, Mario Camerini, to cast the popular Anna Magnani, the "Nannarella" (a nickname for 'Anna'), the acclaimed performer of cinematic neorealism. She was the first Italian actress to have received, in 1956, the Oscar award for her role in the film "La rosa tatuata" ("*The Rose Tattoo*").

Unfortunately, "Suor Letizia", in spite of the excellent storyline which was also highly dramatic, and in spite of the perfect performances not only of Anna Magnani but also of the other actors, premiered at the Venice Film Festival and was rejected by the selection board. The panel of judges was presided over by the famous Luchino Visconti, another central figure involved in the development of Ischia's image, who had directed the famous actress in two of his films: *Bellissima* ('Beautiful') and *Siamo donne* ('We are women'). Although Anna Magnani had received the Silver Ribbon for her performance, she was not content and rebuked Visconti as an "offender" for not having adequately assessed the quality of the film. It seems, however, that Rizzoli phoned Magnani to congratulate her for the award received, but the angry comments of Magnani with his producer were just as prickly as the ones for Visconti; she told him that he himself could keep the Silver Ribbon because probably in Venice they had not acknowledged Anna Magnani in the same way that America did. She also insinuated with her colorful and well-known Roman dialect that perhaps she had not been bestowed the right reward because the productions on the island of Ischia, bearing Rizzoli's name, had been labeled by the press as tourism products.

Of course, we refuse to believe that Visconti was so obtuse as to deny a deserved award to an actress of such great value simply because they had filmed the movie on a tourist island. We do not believe it is at all a shame if an island, beautiful and loved by all vacationers in the world, appears on brochures of travel agencies. It happens to all of the beautiful and pleasant places on the planet. In fact, the already acclaimed director of "Campane a martello", Luigi Zampa, realized that the island appeared since the early 1900s in encyclopedias, in illustrated guides, and in weekly magazines as the *Maga Ischia (the enchantress Ischia)*, the most beautiful island of Campania, and it was praised for the quality of its thermal waters and as for being an extraordinary spot for a vacation and for enjoying its beautiful panoramic views. It was inevitable that the "those in charge", experts from the film world, would ensure they wouldn't miss the opportunity to make films in this brilliant jewel of the Gulf of Naples, realizing the great potential that the location offered at the aesthetic and artistic levels and also the possible effects on the grounds of economic success.

The directors and producers, moreover, were also subjected to the charm of the historical-mythological "memories" of the classical Mediterranean which were also endorsed by the various archaeological finds that always attributed to Ischia a "central" trait in its identity. An example is the story of the travels of Ulysses, in which the island is an important stop-over in the perilous journey of the hero Homer, returning from a long-running and bloody war.

On the other hand, although the island affords natural charm, before becoming the delightful, welcoming place of our day, it was also, as was the case in many areas of southern Italy (See Galasso, 1977), a place of misery, backwardness and deprivation. This was the case at least until its economic and tourist boom. Before benefits from the boom were realized, the situation in Ischia was very different from the one we know today.

"Here it is worse than in Africa, sisters." This is an exclamation, uttered by Anna Magnani, dressed as a nun in one of the key sequences of "Sister Letizia". It is a sequence that shows the arrival of the nuns on the island and their impact with the harsh realities of the new "mission". In short, the phrase is very indicative of the precarious living conditions that were recorded on the island, even after World War II. The star of the film is the little Salvatore, a child abandoned by his family because of the inability to raise him. Little by little he enters the heart of the nun, who, to assure him a stable place in which to live, decides to not sell the convent as she planned to do, and ends up striving to also provide basic necessities to the other inhabitants of the island who were so poor that they couldn't afford anything.

The framework of the conditions of indigenous life is, in fact, simply agonizing. The islanders try to tear from the earth something to provide a livelihood, the fishermen are so poor they do not even have the money to buy the nets, children are dedicated to the theft of a few goats grazing, just to survive; emigration is the only escape from a reality that is too ungenerous, from a world without prospects. One sets out in search of a better life.

The images of the film show an island, then, entirely devoid of any signs of tourism. Sister Letizia gets off the steamboat, in a context of genuine poverty and desolation. But the protagonist in no time identifies the real goal that needs to be achieved, she sets a plan to be implemented and applies a strong will and great determination.

Maybe it is not unreasonable to imagine a possible similarity between the role of "Sister Letizia" and the project that she embodies, and the ideology of the movie's "producer". The nun arrives on the island like a presence that is ready to assist in a context of serious difficulties, clearly shown by the critical situation prevailing in the convent. She is a woman of character, accustomed to face any kind of discomfort, a person able to motivate others, to convey faith, to organize the commitment of the people around her.

Even Angelo Rizzoli, the valiant *Martinitt,* moves, in real life, on the same grounds, pledging to promote the potentiality of the island, appealing strongly to the island's capabilities and to the need for islanders to rely on their own strength. Of significance is his rejection of "extraordinary" interventions, to the point of being indifferent to the financial opportunities offered by the Cassa per il Mezzogiorno (Fund for the South) (Morgera, 2002). In the figure of this legendary industrialist were combined a certain swagger, but also a remarkable practical sense that stemmed from the long experience of his 'working his way up'. A bit in the manner of Sister Letizia, he developed his skills with practice and with work "in the field." He was a man who had graduated from the 'university of the streets', with the highest grades and even praise.

3.3 The Caribbean Gulf: the island of the pirates

Fairy tales usually begin with words full of magic and mystery, as with "once upon a time", which evoke a time and a place alien and distant: remote islands in the seas, brave heroes, risky deeds, keys of a secret world that is parallel to the one in which we are "forced" to live. A fairy-tale world that is adventurous and reaches the limits of imagination, it is where you fly on the wings of imagination, it is an imaginary universe from which the cinema, since its origins, has fully drawn from. It has done so to the point of creating a truly thematic strand, a genre in which extreme freedom is granted and you can make assumptions "up to the borders of reality". Paradoxical adventures, sometimes entirely unrealistic, experienced by heroes adept at maneuvering with cape and sword, paladins who struggle for justice, for the triumph of good and the defeat of the "bad guys." There are also galleons crossing the seas, going from island to island, ship attacks, battles, escapes, poignant love, intense and mutual desires, or burning passions, and unrequited feelings. There are stories that end tragically, or dreams that are ultimately crowned with everyone living happily ever after.

But there are also terrible adventures with hordes of bad guys, of tremendous sailors aboard ships, terrorizing anyone who sees their sails on the horizon. They are terrible men with bandages or black bandanas over one eye, a wooden leg seen here and there, hooks and white skulls painted on the black flags. Ischia, over the centuries, has been endlessly invaded, looted and plundered by Saracen pirates and more. It is no coincidence that amongst the inhabitants of Forio, who were the most exposed islanders to attacks, the phrase "Turkish blood" is still used to refer to themselves.

Because of its appearance, its attractive geographical location, and the existence of real pirates, it was inevitable that Ischia became a greedy bite even for the piracy of films. The first film, inspired by this genre and filmed on the island, is "**Il corsaro nero**" *("The Black Pirate"),* based on the novel by Emilio Salgari and realized in 1936 under the direction of Hamlet Palermi.

The film was reasonably successful and attracted the attention of viewers and critics to the splendid settings of Ischia. It has been said on several occasions that *"The Black Pirate"* had the ability to call back, for the first time, the attention of an audience that was much wider compared to the usual number of movie-goers of the island. The main moment of the film was the long sequence in which Ciro Verratti, Lord of Ventimiglia, rode on the sand of the beautiful beach of Maronti, a beach that was for the first time presented to a wide audience of potential new tourists of the island. The *"Black Pirate"* was followed by other Italian and foreign films of the same genre, and all have contributed significantly to Ischia's familiarity in the world (Deuringer, 1963).

It was probably at a later date that even the director Primo Zeglio would be inspired by the famous novel by Salgari to make the film "**Morgan il pirata**" (1960). The preferred locations of this film are the Punta Molino area, Ischia Ponte, Lacco Ameno and the beach of Maronti, perfect settings for battles scenes between pirates. Despite the beautiful scenery, the film was considered "a ridiculous adventure film," supervised by André de Toth, that was a play on 'accumulation—an accumulation of people, facts and actions—in order to mask the void on which it rested. (Mereghetti, 2002, p.1345). In other words, even when the criticism was fairly merciless when the film was compared with other films filmed on Ischia (criticism was based on the film's poor theme and weak narrative structure), the film still indisputably saved the island's reputation for its impressively beautiful settings. And it is on the basis of these considerations that it seems appropriate to reiterate the importance that was held in having certain film works have settings on Ischia. We could assert without any doubt that, in some cases, the real star of the film is simply the island.

Another film that is not of inferior calibre and is the

same genre is **"Il corsaro dell'isola verde"** (*"The Pirate of the Green Island"*), created in 1952 under the direction of Robert Siodmak.

The reason why the director chose Ischia to create his film seems to refer to a type of rumor on the existence of special chromatic shades present in island environments. In short, what served as the final toward choosing Ischia as the production location for the film was the fact that most people in general dreaded the possibility of experimenting with the use of color. At the time it was discovered that in the island's atmosphere there were very original colors and contrasts which would pose a challenge if one wanted to impress them on film. The ability to pick them up was considered a revolutionary milestone in the realization of film techniques (See Chestnut, 1990, p.165).

It was Ken Adams, assistant set designer at the time of this film's production, who pointed out to the director this interesting and rare peculiarity and who identified the best places on the island for the making of this film. Among the various proposals for the settings, he chose, in agreement with the production staff, the ancient village of Celsa with its Aragonese Castle, the Sant'Anna rocks, the former beach of the Stradone and the 'Piazzale delle Alghe' *(the square of algae)*--settings which made the movie gain rapid success. One can see these places in a historical sequence of the film in which there is a hot-air balloon that traverses the stretch between the Castle and the coastal slope of Soronzano, facing the Cartaromana bay; other scenes were filmed in England instead.

With his first film, Ken Adam acquired a certain reputation, but so did Ischia, thanks to the widespread diffusion of the film throughout American networks; the movie received remarkable feedback on the images. The film helped Ischia jump out of Italy and be exposed to the whole world.

"The islanders were already dreaming of caravans of tourists, attracted by the fame of the exceptional 'colour phenomenon'. They already saw soundstages and facilities being built because one thing was certain: Ischia's air could never be brought to the movie theatres in Hollywood or Cinecittà, bottled like white wine from Mount Epomeo. Instead, films would have to be filmed on the island of Ischia so that they could capture the unique colors (which after all would not cost anything) but leave behind fame and money for the island" (Castagna, 1990, p. 165).

In short, the film's "pirates" who had historically arrived on the island with the intent to pillage, were proving to be this time real benefactors. Obviously, they were not real pirates, as their identity was often falsified and grotesque. Even in the story, rather than being fearsome sea terrorists they were the parody of such. It is a matter which is well understood via the comments Valerio Caprara (2002) has made on the theme: "The subject then, more comical than adventurous, becomes the excuse to unleash stalwart buccaneers in the backgrounds of an incomparable sea: the fifteen minutes of gymnastic feats that closed the film is spectacular—it communicates today's nostalgia for a young, primitive and naïve movie industry."

In this regard, one must consider the manner in which the main actor, American Burt Lancaster, who also produced the film, found the necessary money. For Brian Real, connoisseur of movie themes, "one of the reasons why it was possible to shoot 'The Crimson Pirate' between the island of Ischia and England was because at the time when a film production took place outside the United States one was obligated to reinvest a percentage of the profits in the country of the film's production. It was a constraint that reduced from the get-go the gains that a film could achieve. There was, in short, the need to limit to the maximum the production costs. One method was to choose locations that allowed for reduced charges. Sure, there was some legal and bureaucratic problems overcome, but the savings, including the consideration of taxes, appeared to be significant, and therefore the determinant of one site over another. Ischia owes part of its film popularity also to economic reasons. So, as for the big American productions of Cinecittà, Lancaster found the money for the production of his film. From the standpoint of bargaining power, the Italian trade unions of the fifties and sixties were weaker than those of the United States as a result of a lower level of protection of workers (let's not forget that in Italy it wasn't until the 1990s that show business workers achieved a regularization as well as recognition of their work status, [editor's note]) which meant it was less expensive to shoot films in Italy.

This state of affairs must have almost certainly affected even the production and budget plans of other films, including "Cleopatra," and perhaps even "Fox Hunting" (Real, 2006)

For the making of the film ""Il corsaro dell'isola verde," many extras were needed; for this reason, in the summer of 1952 many islanders were diverted from their usual chores to dress up in bright-colored costumes and vintage uniforms and climbed aboard their fishing boats to take part in the naval battles.

The film is considered a classic of the pirate genre, with a more marked vein of humor and joy. The film's success is certainly attributed to Lancaster's performance which possessed all the characteristics relevant to the character he played: a very tall man who was athletic, blond and blue-eyed with an irresistible smile; he embodied the very figure of the likeable hero and scoundrel that the audience expected. What probably helped him such success was just the fact that he had worked, when he was a young man, in a circus as an acrobat and trapeze artist with his friend Nick Cravat, with whom, in addition to this film, he had already worked on the film "La leggenda dell'arciere di fuoco" ("*The Legend of the fire archer* ")(1950). In any case, these two productions allowed the two actors to become a true legend of world of cinema.

Let's suppose that Lancaster had a lot of fun playing the hero, the outgoing and charming Captain Vallo who was able to twirl on the yards of the ship as a true acrobat. The beginning of the film is pleasant as it anticipates the opening credits, a feature that was typical of *films of those years. Our Captain Vallo swoops on a flying flagpole attached to a rope and says, "You believe only what you will see ... actually, half of what you will see.* " Then, as a good seducer he makes the daughter of the governor fall in love with him and sides with a rebel leader to fight the dictator of the moment. After he is taken as a prisoner, he escapes by walking into the sea, breathing under a capsized boat. Unforgettable is his former companion of acrobatics, the little deaf-mute (Cravat), who is chased by soldiers while he runs away, walking on the ropes and doing somersaults in the streets rebuilt by Warner Brothers. With the help of his friend, our friend finally not only wins back the hand of the "beauty" but he also wins back the galleon he had lost after a splendid swim underwater--a swim which gives us the chance to admire also some beautiful backdrops of Ischia, ."Il corsaro dell'isola verde" is a key moment in the construction of the "modern" myth of Ischia. On the island there are many who still remember episodes and anecdotes from that period.

The restaurant owner **Aniello Di Scala**, the body double of Burt Lancaster, is commonly known by the nickname "Aniello Dai Tu", probably because of his habitual fist-fighting; his commentary is emblematic. Remember the movie was filmed during a fairly difficult period for the islanders: "a few years had passed since the war - he says - and the islanders had not yet recovered from the terrible crisis of those years". The daily income for many indigenous people depended on the participation in the films as extras. But he was privileged; in fact, as a stunt double for Burt Lancaster in the underwater scenes he received 10,000 lire, and when he fist-fought on land he received 5,000 lire. Certainly, for many islanders who had families, the money earned from the film was a godsend: many were able to buy oil for the whole year and Aniello remembers having bought various household objects, even bedframes. He adds that some people, even if they couldn't swim, would still jump into the water, at risk of drowning, to do a movie scene in order to receive the expected remuneration and meal bag. He remembers that movie shootings lasted six or seven months with scenes being shot in Ischia Ponte, mainly on the main road, in Sant'Angelo, Forio, and the Soccorso (a church in Forio). The economic conditions of the islanders were supposedly not prosperous, and Aniello remembers that everyone at the end of a film, would try to get something that was used during the shootings: some shoes, some clothes. So far the story was told by Aniello Di Scala, but between the various commentaries collected there are several others which appear to us as unique and significant. During lunch breaks, **Franco the boatman**, for example, along with other boys his age, would watch the actors eat, waiting for them to throw to them some food.

Franco recalls that the artists really enjoyed seeing the boys' frantic fights that they engaged in among themselves over an opportunity to hoard a few bites of something.

During the production of the film, **the old fisherman Camillo** noticed under his balcony a pile of wood would be piled. During the night, he little by little took possession of the wood and with it he built a boat that allowed him to fish and therefore work for about 30 years.

This not only reveals the quality of wood that was used for shooting movies, but also the very difficult living conditions of the time in which those who had a boat could eat while the others were still having difficulty surviving. But the islanders were not the only ones who experienced a relationship with suffering, for the islanders remember the love that Burt Lancaster had for his own son who was paralyzed by polio. Every day the actor took him on his huge shoulders and carried him to the shore so that he could swim in the sea throughout the entire filming period. Professor Domenico Castagna, a great teacher of the middle school Scotti of Ischia, involved his students in an interesting research study about the films shot on the island. We want to propose here two commentaries of considerable significance that were collected by the students.

Captain **Malfermo Pacifico** said: "I had already been working for a while aboard various vessels, including the galleon of the film, as captain, but when they selected the extras, I agreed to be the lookout of the pirate ship, a wonderful "schooner ". In compensation I received about 150,000 lire, a fairly substantial figure, because few were willing to climb so high to perform that task. Other extras, that challenged themselves in less risky roles, earned, in fact, much less. The real crew used to work "behind the scenes", allowing the ships to move. After a long period of maintenance in the shipyard of the port of Ischia, I, playing the role of captain, and the rest of the crew, returned the ships to Malta to their English owners. The engine was only used for maneuvres made in the ports, while the rest of the navigation was done sailing. It took more than a week to reach the destination."

The story of **Giovan Giuseppe Di Leva** is also interesting: "When I was shooting the film, I was hired for a minor role, to impersonate one of the rowers. The extras being sought had to be youth over the age of eighteen who were at least 1.70 m high to which were offered 2,000 lire a day. In those days that was a more than decent pay. The war had just ended and hunger was everywhere. Since the word about the high compensation spread, a large number of suitable boys for the extras would come forward, and this brought down the pay to 800 lire. In order to train the extras, the producers set up a training ground in the Pineta Mazzella, in Punta Molino, and they rented the hotel "Regina Palace" to gather the actors together. The shootings lasted for several months. The main scenes were filmed mostly off of the Castello, on an ancient galleon and some boats would shuttle between the land and the ship. Moreover, on the square of the algae a stage was set up for musicians as well as a big barn out of which came a hot air balloon. Instead, at the Stradone and the Soccorso a crenellated pillbox was built from which attacks from the sea were rejected and from where many scenes were shot. "

For the entire work period the entire film crew stayed at the hotel "Queen's Palace" where at the end of the work day the extras would queue to collect their pay. The shooting continued until October. Meanwhile, in the context of the island, the female protagonist of the film was the actress Eva Bartok who made Totò 'crazy for her' to the point that he dedicated to her the famous song: "Ischia mia" ("*My Ischia*"), commonly known as "*Ischia, paravis' e gioventù*" ("*Ischia, paradise and youth"*).

Riccardo D'Ambra recalls that this film marked the beginning of the building of piers and docks, even though ship equipment was fairly new, which allowed for a significant improvement of Ischia's sea links with the mainland. Born in 1946, he remembers that at that time the island's port was not accessible by ship; a ship would stop at the pier and the passengers would cross board over to row boats with which one would finally reach the land. It was with this movie that Agostino Lauro, the first tourist ship owner of the island, brought the production crew around. He earned the money needed to buy the first tourist ship, "la freccia" ("*the arrow*"), which could ferry as many as 25 people.

Andrea Impagliazzo, owner of another historical bar of the island "Il giardino degli aranci" *("The orange garden"*) recalls another piece of historical memory that links Ischia to the world of cinema. Called to play minor roles in many films, it was in this movie that he played a special character. He smiled, slyly, while thinking back to when he was training, behind the pine forest of "Rancio Fellone" together with Burt Lancaster, with ropes and tents over which he had to jump. He remembers having jumped countless times on the deck of a ship 28 meters long. His compensation amounted to 8000 lire a day and shooting lasted 3-4 weeks. As we can see, around the "historical" events associated with the realization of "Il corsaro dell'isola verde" survives a mutually shared living memory on Ischia of a time that perhaps changed the destiny of the island.

3.3.1 Dispersed films

But it is interesting to note that in the memory of many extras who worked on several other film productions, special memories emerge such as anecdotes unknown to most. There are even discovered films that were regularly filmed and of which almost nobody knows about.
The search for movies based on their location is difficult, because in previous years special importance to this aspect was not given. Often the locations of a film were not even recorded anywhere, not to mention the foreign productions of which it is almost impossible "to get to the bottom of" the information regarding the location. In the memoirs of **Andrea Impagliazzo**, for example, there are two films in which claims to have personally participated as a special character: **"Manuele il guardaboschi"** ("*Manuele the forester*"), a film directed by Tony Sailer in 1962, shot outdoors between Ischia and Sant'Angelo and indoors in Germany. In 1963 he was in the movie **"L'isola"** of which he does not remember the plot but he does remember that he had been the protagonist for a few minutes. **Peppe Iacono**, nicknamed "il biondo" ("*the blonde guy*") is famous for having played one of the gladiators in the famous movie "Cleopatra", a movie which will be discussed elsewhere. He too has many memories to narrate; in fact, many parts of his commentary even circulate via the web. It is he who talks about the German production of the film "**La bella pastorella**" ("*The beautiful shepherdess*"), filmed between Panza and Sant'Angelo, a movie in which Peppe was an extra. Unfortunately, even traces of this film seem to have gone missing.

3.4 The island of horrors

The echoes of the bombing of World War II had just turned off, Ischia was beginning to recover from a period of grief and terrible hardships. It was 1945 and the crew involved in the making of the film **"Il vampiro dell'isola"** (*"The island vampire"*) landed in Ischia's harbor. The film, directed by Mark Robson, is set in 1912 and tells the story of a group of people who discover that among the inhabitants of their island lies a murderess whose soul is possessed by an evil spirit. Another movie that is somewhat of a horror film is **"Il Mostro dell'isola"** (*"Monster Island"*) filmed in 1953 and directed by Roberto Bianco Montero. The plot tells the story of a police officer who discovers illegal trafficking managed by a powerful local character. But this man, a person who appears to be innocent, is finally under investigation (thanks to the officer) and makes arrangements to take revenge on him and intimidate him by kidnapping his daughter. Luckily, with the help of a woman who had been an accomplice of the crimes that were part of the investigation, the officer finds his daughter and serves justice.

In this film the island shows its face as one that is quite unprecedented, it is an Ischia that is a times gloomy, Gothic, made of secret crannies, and chains of darkness that arouse feelings of pure anguish and very intensively generate what today would be called "suspense ". One has said that the island is the location of the two films, but it pains to point out that this is not mentioned in either case, although individual sites chosen as the setting for the scenic actions are well recognizable. The protagonist of the two films is the famous British actor Boris Karloff, one of the legends of horror films; he is a figure who has left an indelible mark in the world of fictional classic films. That icon of the corpulent, lurching monster with a scarred face has gone down in as Frankenstein.

3.5 The island of crime drama: The Mongibello by Patricia Highsmith

In 1959 in Ischia the movie "**Delitto in pieno sole**" ("*Purple Noon*") was filmed and directed by Rene Clement. The lead role was entrusted to Alain Delon who was twenty-four years old at the time. He plays a character with an angelic face, but possesses a 'demonic soul. Thanks to this production, Delon had the opportunity to learn about the great director Luchino Visconti, who, at that time was looking for the protagonist of his movie "Rocco e i suoi fratelli" ("*Rocco and His Brothers"*). This film was inspired by a beautiful novel by Patricia Highsmith. This author gives life to a singular character: an ambiguous, fake man who lives off of scams and does not hesitate to assassinate a friend of his in order to improve his social position. Neither Ischia nor Procida are cited as a location, but to satisfy Highsmith's desire to have the novel's setting in Positano and therefore in the Gulf of Naples, the location is given a fancy name: Mongibello. In fact, a town with this name exists, but Mongibello is another name used to describe the Etna. About forty years later, in 1998, Anthony Minghella, filmed the remake of the same film entitled "Il talento di Mr. Ripley" ("The Talented Mr. Ripley") by using Ischia again for film shoots. While realizing the same plot and narrative, film-like patterns, Clement and Minghella developed two versions of the same character, starting with the homosexual tendencies of the protagonist which in Clement's film was far less pronounced. This is justified, probably, with the prevailing conformism of the 1950s, the historical period that hardly allowed for explicit references to the sexual characteristics of characters that expressed a "different" trait. Clement remains vague even with regard to the geographical habitat, and offers the viewer the opportunity to imagine the setting of the story as any place that could be related to one's to hermeneutics and to one's own sensitivity. Nevertheless this "abstraction" is realized by respecting the landscaped surroundings in which the movie was made, its specific orographic connotation. The identity of the site, in short, is simply hidden and is never entirely shown: several scenes only portray the pier of Ischia Ponte with the ancient houses of the Borgo of Celsa in the background; these homes are positioned on the opposite side of the Aragonese Castle. At the end of the movie, the protagonist relaxes while sunbathing on the Maronti beach, with the scenery of the Sant'Angelo promontory in the distance. Minghella's film, however, has attempted to reconstruct the image of 1957 Italy, but be seems to have been unsuccessful in doing so, partly because of some unforgivable weaknesses: what appear in some of the sequences are books of the publishing house Adelphi and records of Miles Davis and John Coltrane, all published in periods after that of the film's setting (Mereghetti, 2002). However, unlike Clement's film, Minghella clearly lets the islands of Ischia and Procida stand out, and he also explicitly emphasizes the pleasure of living in this place when the villagers sing: "This is the most beautiful country in the world". Among other proposed scenarios we find the beach club area which includes the characteristic Bagno Antonio and the Vico Marina; here there is the portrayal of a popular, typically Southern festival, with sheets and blankets spread out from balconies and a Madonna emerging from the sea. It is an evocative portrayal, although not identifiable with the specific folkloric traditions of the island (See Crossbow, 2004, p.89). The end of the movie also allows for several interpretations, somewhat of a "cliff-hanger" caused by the restlessness of the protagonist. The comparison between the two productions seem to confirm what is expressed by the critics, that is, Minghella's film is substantially inferior to that of Clement.

3.6 Blockbuster Ischia: "Cleopatra"

The 60s witness the heavy lean of the historical-adventure genre on the international film scene; this genre is later identified as " peplum style". In cases in which there was an expenditure of resources, the media impact of the new shooting technique in Cinemascope, which was also a blockbuster, was exploited. Among these movies, the production that made the most headlines for a number of reasons that we shall soon see, was a grandiose costume drama with some historical claim, a blockbuster indeed entitled "Cleopatra", directed by Joseph L. Mankiewicz. In this film many scenes were filmed on the green island. The story of the Egyptian queen and her lovers winds its way up to its tragic end with the backdrop of some of the most extraordinary environments of Ischia, starting from the majestic Aragonese Castle, used as a setting for the battle of Anzio. Unfortunately, the island, although shown from many angles and is absolutely unmistakably identifiable, is basically not even mentioned as the location of the film.

As recalled by some islanders, the arrival of directors in Ischia for filming is probably due to John Messina who was at the time the manager of organizing local filmmaking. He helped filmmakers overcome various difficulties related to film production, resolved any bureaucratic obstacles to obtaining the necessary permits, and selected the extras and scene props. The main actress of the film is the big, beautiful Elizabeth Taylor of the legendary violet eyes. She was a worrisome woman, sensual and dark, capricious and spoiled, with a turbulent private life, with a considerable amount of husbands and probably lovers, and was suffering from an unknown number of illnesses, real or fictitious, of which perhaps one of the most proven concerning serious disorders from which she was suffering was actually her personality. Whatever the case, she was considered the most beautiful woman in the world. Anecdotes on the temper of the diva and the tantrums of her stay in Ischia were widespread. The testimonies gathered about the matters related to the production seem unanimous: the making of the film was a real ordeal. The period of filming seemed endless. Administrators tended to attribute all the problems of the production, starting from the budget overruns, to the crazy demands made by Liz Taylor and the excessive expenses of the crabby diva: about 500,000 lire a week for her hairdresser, 31,000,000 lire for overtime work, 1.89 billion lire for expenses covered by the production for her illness in 1961. Apparently, while Taylor was filming "Hotel International" in London she justified her demands by saying that over the eleven months of filming in Rome she would have had, even according to official calculations of the production, only 11 hours recorded as late, and regarded this as a woman's privilege. With regard to her health, after the serious disease of 1961 in London she stated that she was not sick not even for a day, except for a couple of flus and a one-time mild food poisoning.

Still concerning the complex situations that characterized the production phase, one must take into account some judgment, certainly not flattering, over the behavior of Italians during the period of filming. If you surf the internet you can still find testimonies on the matter. It seems that some of the crew members have reported some unedifying episodes: "we were like bandits who robbed the forest. The money flowed. Taylor reported that the mineral water bill for technicians and actors reached $ 80,000 in eleven months. In order for this expenditure to be justified we should have drunk, each one of us, about ten liters of water a day. "

But what did the islanders remember about this film? The people of Ischia, during the making of the film, were particularly impressed by the fact that on the set on which the love between Marcantonio and Cleopatra was consumed was also where was born the love between Liz and her partner, Richard Burton, who was a protagonist in the movie with her. Rivers of ink flowed in the newspapers about their stormy love; their love story fueled long the gossip columns of all the newspapers of the time. They were both married, and both were divorced from their spouses to marry. Their story of love and passion lasted several years, although always fueled by furious quarrels, colossal drinking and mutual insults. Another aspect that has stuck in the island's memory is the great amount of financial squandering, which was appreciated by some locals. For example, the ease with which money was spent certainly did not displease the owners of caverns and stores. The production spent amounts of money, that were considered exaggerated during that time period, to rent a large number of caverns and storage houses to store the necessary materials for the shooting which were never even used. But the highlight of the gossip still concerns Liz Taylor. The diva, guest of the Regina Isabella Hotel of Lacco Ameno, would have to go to Ischia Porto's Hotel Jolly for make-up. Since this was before the shooting, she often took advantage of the situation to drink some whiskey along the way. The situation often became quite comical. On those occasions, and under conditions which one can only imagine, she actually even sent letters to the poor director, who was waiting with the whole crew in the shooting location in Ischia Ponte, claiming the most diverse reasons for which she was indisposed to act that day.

Tonino Baiocco, well-known celebrity of Ischia's nightlife in its heyday and dear friend of Luchino Visconti, remembers that at the time he was the owner of the restaurant "La Lampara", not yet a discotheque; it was there that he strove to prepare "pocket lunches". At the time no one knew what they were, nor how to prepare them, but because of the need and the desire to meet the production company's order in order to earn some money, they experimented with the preparation. Fortunately, the experiment succeeded, and it turned out in the best way. In the late evening, after working at the restaurant, Baiocco, along with a group of young people, arranged the tables in such a fashion as to facilitate the preparation and created a kind of assembly line so that he could get busy with the preparation of these lunches.

In short, the film production company found itself not only having to deal with the difficult management of the story of a complex historical event, but also that of the turbulent private life of the protagonists, as well as the economic burden of the most expensive film in the history of filmmaking. The film was an enormous success, but despite its nine Academy Award nominations the winning of four awards (photography, set design, costumes, special effects), the production was not able to avoid bankruptcy (Mereghetti, 2002).

As for the consequences that the movie "Cleopatra" had on the island, in spite of everything it was a film whose grandeur had a profound effect on the material life and culture of the island; it was a real milestone for its film history and a formidable economic device, which yielded considerable benefits to Ischia's community, distributing huge resources on the income of the population, giving great life to the island's economy. Moreover, the response that Ischia obtained for its image and for the growth of its international reputation cannot be precisely determined. The testimony of Captain **Silverio Rumore**, obtained by students of Professor Castagna, fully provides proof through this conversation: "I was not yet 18 when the film shooting in Ischia began. For many islanders, as well as for technicians and workers of Cinecittà, as well as for the carpenters of Torre del Greco who saw in their shipyards the light vessels used to shoot scenes of the naval battle, the film was a godsend, a real bonanza. This was not the view taken by Fox, for which the blockbuster cost a fortune and caused Fox's financial meltdown. This film was a blessing even for my family. My father, Vincenzo Rumore, made our first boat available to the production company: San Ciro, and I was the captain. Our task was to take 150 girls every day, the maids of Cleopatra, from the jetty to the Queen's ship, anchored off of Cartaromana, and vice versa. When I ferried, I only did two trips by boarding a number of girls that was superior to the boat's holding capacity; I did this to save fuel.

There were many extras in Ischia, but only 6 or 7 playing the maids were from the island: the Ischitan parents were protective of their daughters and of course did not allow them to appear only covered by a veil. If I think about how girls go around dressed today, I laugh.

At lunch I had the task of bringing the baskets with an abundance of food for the actors and extras. The Hotel Jolly was the hotel that prepared them; There were never less than 500, and they were always so many that were leftover. Some Neapolitan peddlers would take them and resell them in Naples; they too would have some earnings. On the ship "San Ciro" I worked with several other sailors: at the time of negotiating the daily price I thought to ask for 10,000 lire, which to me was already quite a bit. But it was suggested that I ask for more, since Americans would be paying. I asked for 25,000 lire per day and the production managers accepted without question. And to think that the cost of the ticket for a tour of the entire island was then 150 lire! So, with that boat I could collect a maximum of 10,000 lire to tour the island. I basically had a good deal. I remember that everyone was talking about the beauty of Liz Taylor and her budding love for Burton; when her husband arrived on the set from boutique "Dominique", where he had bought the most expensive clothes for her, the beautiful Liz did nothing better than throw them overboard. The famous star had found hospitality on Rizzoli's yacht: La Serena. In the eyes of us mere islanders, that movie, the set design, the costumes and special effects, the lunches, the parties, the money, the expensive cars, the beautiful boats, the million-dollar yacht, left us stunned, with our mouths wide open. It was as if a fairy tale were taking place before our eyes, and we were somehow part of it. "

3.7 The island is promoted

After so much "horror", the films of the second decade after the war opened up to images of unique landscapes. Within a few years the comedy-tourist films helped spread this subgenre to the point that, thanks to the possibility of using more color, the most famous places in the country were enhanced and advertised so that they became a genuine attraction for international tourism. After contemplating the beauty of nature and the island's art, two main elements were emphasized: the tourist landscape, with the representation of a beautiful view of the characteristic traits of a particular location, underlining yet again its beauty, and a gallery of celebrities who in my opinion are observed subliminally and whose roles, entrusted to the protagonists, promote island locations through their own interpretations of young people who are on holiday or who stumbled on the location for various reasons ; that model is itself attractive to lead people to the tourist areas (cf. Brunette, 1998).

The tourism landscape is enhanced especially in the film "Scampolo" (or "Sissi in Ischia" (1957), the trade name in the title of the film that exploited the notoriety achieved by the famous actress as "Princess Sissi"). In "Scampolo", Romy Schneider plays the role of girl from Ischia, named Scampolo, a tourist guide, who shows travelers the island and its beauties, as is the case, in fact, for the tour guides of the island. The film is about the young woman who meets an important architect whose project based on an entire district of Naples meets several obstacles that will be overcome with the help enterprising girl. The film, despite its innocent rhetoric, is all but lacking in quality and has an attractive, pleasant self-confidence, both for its characters, taken from the popular setting, and for the landscape. In any case, this film popularized Ischia even more for the people living north of the Alps and is maybe what brought Schneider and Visconti together (Crossbow, 2004, p. 87). Noteworthy is the pleasant portrayal of Mario Mazzella, reknown and valiant painter of the island, who plays the part of himself. And here is also a notation that concerns one of the two authors of this book, Marianna Sasso: "My grandmother died long before I was born, but I was able to see her in some of the sequences of " Scampolo ", a movie in which she was an extra. It was exciting to see my ancestor reacquire life before my eyes, as if she were among us. " This reveals one of the most characteristic virtues that the old medium of film possesses (as does photography and more), and is now a thing of all imaging technologies: to bring back to life, I dare say magically, not only myths, the stars, the scenes and scenarios of extraordinary impact, but also fragments of authentic everyday life, which can have, for some, intense emotional meaning and great evidential value.

The film crew of "Scampolo" was staying for the duration of the shooting at the Gran Albergo dei Pini and Schneider played the role of a tour guide in the coach of Antonio Califano which was full of extras from Ischia. For the beautiful Austrian actress this was one of many romantic comedies filmed before she met Alain Delon, with whom she was engaged, and before she fully developed an artistic relationship with Luchino Visconti who fully revealed her talent as an actress.

It 's just one of the many beautiful moments of the seduction mechanism that Ischia has activated on the international public. Moreover, the island, at least in the eyes of the Europeans, and above all in those of the Germans, has always had a leading role, not only for its thermal baths, but also for its colors and the hospitality of the islanders; the Germans have always been frequent visitors of the island. Probably Alfred Wiedermann, the German director of "Scampolo", thought that with this production he would be able to bring to the land of Germany a bit of that radiance that is much appreciated by his countrymen. Who knows if perhaps for the author the film's story contained upon close scrutiny a subtle metaphor, to establish a sort of "reconciliation" among peoples whose relationship had been strained with the tragic, controversial events of World War II. As it is, "Scampolo", and several other works of the same style, make up almost a "genre" in their own right that has its own uniform identity, a distinctive trait that can be attributed to its various aspects. As for the structure of the story, this type of film usually tends to place a well-structured gallery of celebrities into a uniform topological dimension. Narrative stories, in short, occur via a romantic tourist route, which brings together people from different social backgrounds, who share moments of being together as a group and moments of seduction (See Brunette, 1998). In this narrative a variety of elements are realized: the comedy of customs, the comedy genre or drama. Social and political topics of interest often are combined with events translated into a satirical tone and backed up by appropriate locations. In Ischia these type of productions have for a long period of time been supported and sponsored by the production company "Cineriz" founded by the entrepreneur Angelo Rizzoli; this strongly promotes the island on the tourist level, worldwide.

In 1962, the film Leoni al sole "Lions in the Sun", directed by Vittorio Caprioli, had a part of it shot in Ischia. It is about the daily misadventures of a group of young Neapolitans on holiday in Positano (See

Crossbow, 2004). The film is significant primarily because it was vaguely inspired by a remarkable work about Naples in the 1950s, written by Raffaele La Capria. Wounded to death, he was a brave Neapolitan writer who also coscripted the film.

3.7.1 The adventures of Cineriz

The cinematic production of Rizzoli stands out primarily because it has been very copious. Within a few years, "Cineriz" produces, in Ischia, a series of films that achieve discrete and even remarkable commercial successes. On the aesthetic quality of this production, controversial and very strict judgments arise. It should be noted that works of film always deserve to be valued individually and not as a group. That being said, it is clear that it dealt mainly with light works, which sometimes included the widest line in Italian comedy and that aimed at mass audiences, essentially searching for moments of entertainment and evasion.
Lacrime d'amore ("*Tears of Love*") is made by Cineriz in 1954, directed by Mario Amendola. Some scenes of the film were shot at Ischia Ponte on Rizzoli's yacht, il Sereno. The story tells of a burning adventure between the wife of an industrialist and a Neapolitan singer. The two lovers leave their families to live their lives, but the woman tries to escape desperately from the passionate charm of her passion, returning to her life. **Vacanze a Ischia** ("*Vacations in Ischia*"), directed by Mario Camerini in 1956, depicts its narrative episodes with the background of Lacco Ameno's Hotel Regina Isabella and its spas, the characteristic tuff mushroom, and the marvelous blue sea. The film contains several interwoven beach resort episodes: that of a young

French woman, played by Myriam Bru, tried for a presumed outrage over modesty; the crisis of an engineer, impersonated by Vittorio De Sica, convinced that his wife is betraying him; the guilty conscience of a tourist, Nino Besozzi, sure to be responsible for the death of a little boy who jumped into the sea to retrieve a coin.

But among the productions of Cineriz is remembered the film **Suor Letizia** ("*Sister Letizia*") (1957), played by Magnani, of which we have already spoken extensively. **Appuntamento ad Ischia** ("*An Appointment in Ischia*"), a work of 1960 under the direction of Mario Mattoli, is played by a rich cast: Domenico Modugno, Ciccio Ingrassia, Franco Franchi, Mina and Pippo Franco. In the movie Modugno, in the shoes of a famous singer, is a widower and has a daughter, Letizia, to whom he wants to give a mother. But the girl does not accept her father's companion, for she would prefer he grow fond of Mirella, another young woman she would like as a mother. The girl, in order to realize her wish, creates different situations (for example, she convinces her father to go to Ischia for spa treatments, at the spas of la Regina Isabella), to let her father and Mirella meet and fall in love. Of course, in this case the privileged locations are those of the municipality of Lacco Ameno, with a beautiful seafront scene of the boardwalk connecting Lacco Ameno and Casamicciola Terme and traversed by carriage by Modugno and his daughter. Among the celebrities in the film, besides Modugno, there is the famous Mina who sings **Un cielo in una stanza** ("*A Sky in a Room*") and **Una zebra a pois** ("*A spotted Zebra* "). Significant is the fact that Franco Franchi and Ciccio Ingrassia debut in the film, with their naif comedy, based on grimaces and impudent imitations of Jerry Lewis (Bassoli, 1987). The director proposed to the couple who would become so famous in national comedy to play the role of two ferocious smugglers. Franco and Ciccio were engaged for the roles for the sum of £ 50,000, with travel to Ischia at their own expense, for a total commitment of 13 days. It was in this way that their first movie experience was born on "the green island".

1966, however, is the year of production of **Ischia amore operazione** under the direction of Vittorio Sala. The film is of some importance, that being the fact that it welcomes the movie debut of the comedians Ric and Gian. The plot is very simple: Peppino De Filippo, in the shoes of Gennaro Capatosta, runs an inn offering full board together with his wife and children. The fact is that the innkeeper's children (a barber, a boutique owner, and a calloused "don Giovanni"), provide the hotel's customers with every kind of service. The main settings are in the enchanting scenery of Sant'Angelo; other locations are the Soccorso of Forio and the Guevara Tower in Ischia that serve as backgrounds for seduction and love scenes. The main filmmaker is Walter Chiari, a great friend of Rizzoli, who had made his film debut in the late 1940s. Peppino De Filippo, however, played a second-tier role. In the plot is also Tony Renis playing the role of a genius. Various scenes in which he appears are set up instead in the town of Lacco Ameno, the main location being the hotel "Regina Isabella" where Walter Chiari stays. But during this period of cinema in Ischia it is very interesting to recall the direct memory of an outstanding protagonist: Tony Renis. We meet him at the "Regina Isabella" bar. He is always a nice, talkative, helpful and well-mannered artist. In his words, one collects the echoes of a context and of a phase of great significance in the cultural, spectacular and worldly affair of the island

and its golden age.

3.7.2 When When You Will Come ...... to Ischia

Mister Renis, how did you, as a singer, encounter the world of cinema?

"The first film I participated in as a co-star was called "Io bacio, tu baci" (I kiss, you kiss). I acted in it with Mina in 1958, along with Umberto Orsini, Jimmy Fontana and Gianni Meccia. It was, in essence, a musical film, and we had Adriano Celentano as a guest of honour. Even among the extras there were characters destined to become real stars: Raffaella Carrà, Franco Califano, Angelo Infranti and Vittorio Gassman's wife: Diletta D'Andrea."

How did you meet Angelo Rizzoli?

"My debut took place in 1962 in San Remo with the song "Quando, quando quando". Rizzoli, who was staying at the Royal Hotel, contacted me for the movie 'Accadde in Riviera' (" It Happened in the Riviera ") that then transformed into "Appuntamento in Riviera" (" An Appointment in Riviera"). The film was shot almost all over Italy: Rome, Cortina d'Ampezzo, Chioggia, Intra and Pallanza, San Remo. Movie titles at that time often changed because the writers began in a way and then changed their mind (...) Walter Chiari and I were the pupils of Angelo Rizzoli. A good relationship existed between us, the commendatore loved us very much. The cinema of the era was "pure and simple", the period between the late 1950s and the 1960s and 1970s, representing the golden age of musical films which were vaguely inspired by the American style, the singers like Elvis.

Ischia was the real capital of a certain kind of cinema; it seduced many directors. At that time, it was very fashionable to come to Ischia. The greatest merit of the popularity that the island had acquired in those years was certainly attributed to Rizzoli, a great publisher and filmmaker.

What memory do you have of Ischia and what did the islanders look like when the film Ischia operazione amore ("Ischia Love operation") was filmed?

I remember a simply beautiful Ischia, now it's a bit changed, but it's still gorgeous. I remember a place in Ischia where I often went: "Il Rancio fellone" where I enjoyed listening to singer Ugo Calise.
The island seemed to me to have been crossed by some well-being, the people seemed to live in a climate of relative serenity. When the film was shot, Ischia was, in certain respects, much more famous than Capri, especially thanks to the situation set in motion by Angelo Rizzoli. Today one tends to forget it, but the work done by the commendatore brought great value to the island territory.

What reminds you of the movie you shot at Ischia?

The films of the time were often in episodes. There were so many small mini movies put together. I played the role of Marco, I remember as if it were now, a nuclear engineer who thought he would make extraordinary discoveries but instead had one failure after another. Walter Chiari played the role of a failed footballer and his only interest was women. Everything took place around an inn run by Peppino de Filippo, a place from which a few stories developed. In the film I also sang a song of mine: "Nessun'altra che te" - the artist at this point even mentions some verses - "for as long as I live. I do not ask for anything, I already have everything, I have you. "The lyrics were by Mogol, Alberto Testa and Vito Pallavicini. Today, a remake of this song is recorded in the CD by Bobby Solo and Little Tony. The film took 7 weeks to make with shots in this hotel (Regina Isabella) and at Sant'Angelo. I remember having lived those weeks very intensely. The artist still browses the photo album of memories, perhaps he is moved. "I do not know if we will go down in history with those movies, but believe me, Cineriz did a really good job at that time."

*Another achievement of Cineriz was "**Diciottenni al sole**" ("Teens in the Sun") filmed in 1962 by director Camillo Mastrocinque with Catherine Spaak and Gianni Garko. The plot is casual: some young people who come to Ischia for a weekend take advantage of their free time to chase women, but being lovers of gambling, these young people lose a large sum of money and are forced to make hubs on the ferryboat of their creditor (...) There are many songs included in the film: "Nicole", "Donna da morire" ("Woman to die"), "Twist n° 9", "Pinne fucili ed occhiali" ("Fins, rifles and glasses"), Guarda come dondolo ("Look at how I swing"). It is said that while filming the film, the protagonists Catherine Spaak and Fabrizio Cappucci were caught off guard by the set designer Aurelio Brugnola while being amorous on the Maronti beach. Later they married, but their union lasted only for a short time. Spaak then married singer Johnny Dorelli.*
After this series of very "light" films promoted and funded by Cineriz, the cinematic production on the island continues with 'thicker' films, sometimes due

*to their derivation from precious theatrical texts and the involvement of directors, writers and actors who at the time were already famous. This is the case of the film "**Caccia alla volpe**" ("Fox hunting") in 1966, taken from the comedy by Neil Simon, directed by Vittorio De Sica and the collaboration of Cesare Zavattini. Among the main actors were Peter Sellers, Victor Mature, Paolo Stoppa and Vittorio De Sica, director of himself, as was his usual habit. For the delightful village of Sant'Angelo, the film obtained a great advertising impact, which remarkably affected the economy of the municipality of Serrara Fontana of which Sant'Angelo is the small seaside village. The village, still tied to agriculture, was not readily accessible due to its high geographic position and its distance from the sea; it was basically poor even after the economic boom that had hit the rest of the island. The protagonist is a robber, "la volpe" ("the fox"), who must leave his mark as a successful thief. The thief is played by Peter Sellers, an actor who already had his hilarious successes, such as "Il Dottor Stranamore" ("Dr. Strangelove") and "La Pantera Rosa" ("The Pink Panther). The press was not very favorable toward De Sica, accusing him of falling into the commercial genre. Apart from the aesthetic issues, the work of the film influenced the economy of Serrara Fontana quite a bit, an economy which was essentially focused on agriculture. There were a few buses, the people lived off of products from the land and raised livestock. As for tourism, it never developed here as it did on the rest of the island, not even today.*

The testimony of **Rosanna Iacono**, collected by the students of the Scotti Institute, is very significant to understand how the event of film production was experienced in a place not yet used to such situations, as was the case in Porto d'Ischia and Lacco Ameno. Rosanna was also among the extras that ran on the beach just as the director said. De Sica was a great worker, ready to advise and even reprimand actors, technicians and extras when they did not follow his orders well. Sometimes he even used very strong language.

Sant'Angelo, then a fishing village that was turning into a delightful tourist harbor, for some days became a site that reminded us of ancient, essential and fascinating places. Farmers and fishermen for a week became actors and inhabitants of Sevalio. Those who were older now cannot testify to their experience, but those who were young at that time are still alive. When reviewing the film, Rosanna was very excited; she went back in time for a moment as a carefree teenager, a rascal who was proud about having earned in one day as much as her father had earned in a week of hard work. She regrets not having any photos of those days spent in Sevalio under the warm sun, but cheerfully and with a sea that was reminiscent of the purity of precious stones, not yet embedded in gold. "Britt Ekland, Maria Grace Buccella, Victor Mature, were nice people, at least then that is how they seemed to me; but Lando Buzzanca was very funny when he grimaced like a brat and ran after the little kids. " Peasants came from Panza, Forio, Fontana to see the movie and remain fascinated--even a little disturbed--because Sant 'Angelo, who had turned into Sevalio, was unrecognizable, as a result of the changes made mainly to the square. All the films shot in Ischia in the 1950s and 1960s helped to make our island known in Italy and Europe, but also helped many families, albeit for a short time, to make ends meet because mainly fathers of families would make movie appearances and earn in a week what they would have earned in two months of work in the field harvesting.

Maria Manieri, a housewife, recalls that at the time she was 24 years old and earned as much as three thousand lire per day (bread costed £ 100 per kilo) as a film extra for three months, from June to July. Sant'Angelo was set up as a museum. Among other things, she had to sing the first famous words of what is considered to be the oldest Neapolitan song, "Michelemmà", with its most famous verses: "he was born in the middle of the sea, Michael, mom's dear son, Michael, mom's dear son, it is an escarole" repeated three times. She remembers Vittorio De Sica and the other actors who came down to Sant'Angelo by horse, and above all, she remembers that with the money she earned, she was finally able to buy a Vespa for her husband.

Even with the movie "**Avanti**", better known as "**Che cosa è successo tra mio padre e tua madre**" *("What Happened Between My Dad and Your Mother")* directed in 1972 by the famous Billy Wilder, author of works of the likes of "Some Like It Hot" and "Irma the sweet", great advertising appeal was earned for Ischia. The film tells of a man in Baltimore who learns of the disappearance of his father in Italy. When he arrives in Ischia to recover his corpse, he discovers that his father died with his lover whose daughter he happens to know; the daughter did not feel like acknowledging their parents' love ...

Only a director with humor, wrote Valerio Caprara (2002), "could capture the rhythm that connects and confuses absurd behaviors, spicy flavors and exhilarating views, does not spare the vices and the paradox of this physical "live and let live" conduct as shown by the cameos of the Trotta brothers with their lazy grinder, the hotel manager, and the gravedigger played by the then unknown Pippo Franco. "

The film is presented like an auto-ironic portrait of what Americans see in the Mediterranean soul, and above all in the European soul. Ischia becomes a location for the description of a case of "therapeutic" infidelity, a place where you can relax and enjoy life. The Chiesa del Soccorso is turned into a morgue where a gangly official (Pippo Franco) has to hurry up with certificates and stamped papers. For the landing of a helicopter the runway of Lacco Ameno was used, a small heliport, also this should be remembered, realized by Angelo Rizzoli. Other shots were made at Sant'Angelo, on Mount Vico where the whole panorama of Lacco Ameno was filmed, then at the port of Ischia, at Ischia Ponte and along the state road leading to Forio. Other scenes, including the one with the hotel where several interiors were set, were shot in Sorrento.

Franco Iavarone is a nice Neapolitan celebrity, a man who was once a tailor and then became an actor. As a self-taught man he has even acted with Fellini in Prova d'orchestra ("Orchestra Test") and, together with Benigni, in "Il Minestrone" by Sergio Citti, 23 years ago.

Recently, he has played Mangiafuoco in the film "Pinocchio", directed by Roberto Benigni. He has been a frequent traveler to the island for many years and remembers that he learned a part in English so that he could be chosen for the movie "Avanti". For him it was very important at the time to have the chance to work with Billy Wilder, a very renowned filmmaker who was the equivalent of Fellini, Antonioni, De Sica. After the interview, he remembers that Wilder seemed to be very amused by him, especially by his English which he defined as "particular", but he did not select Franco for the part.

The disappointment was so great, but it served to increase his determination and give him the energy for a new experience.

It should be noted that for about fifteen years, as of the second half of the seventies, Ischia lived a golden oblivion. That is to say, it enjoyed the income accumulated with the notoriety acquired for the merit of the film production previously made in its territory, but, as we have seen and as we will see, even with low quality thematic films. It should not be forgotten that at that time, Italy passed through a historical period of severe social tension due mainly to the acts of political terrorism carried out by the Red Brigades, followed in the early 1990s by judicial events related to the so-called "Mani pulite"; we will see better in the chapters below the incidence of these phenomena in Ischia and the influences that they have produced. Moreover, European and world film production was disoriented between the search for new "engaging" themes, the forerunner of new creative and production models, and the enjoyment of cassette movies, of mostly erotic sex comedy. There seemed to be almost a clear demarcation between authored movies and the exclusive commercialized cinema. In fact, a generalized crisis in cinema was announced; it was forced to downsize with respect to the television model and to deal with the advent of digital cable and the great possibilities offered by its special effects. Towards the end of the 90s, the trend towards a "light" cinema is, to a certain extent, backed up by new and more rapid shooting techniques. With it there is also the pleasure of the setting which again sees Ischia at the center of attention. Continuing with a "disengaged" production which lacked both the consequences of the previous licentious currents and the easy topics of the 1950s and 1960s, Leonardo Pieraccioni directed **Il Paradiso all'improvviso** ("The paradise suddenly") in 2003. An easy-to-take film in which Pieraccioni plays the role of Lorenzo, a young man who is stubbornly single. He is the owner of a special effects company that produces snow, rain and hail, and is contacted for a supply of this kind in Ischia where the beautiful Amaranta has asked for his services to organize a magical evening with her boyfriend. Everything goes uphill for the desertion of her boyfriend, but since the young woman loves Lorenzo's friendly nature, she decides to seek consolation in him, inviting him to spend the romantic weekend together. Love grows between them, and Lorenzo is fully involved in this love story. What lies behind this whole situation is the fact that it was born out of a challenge presented by Lorenzo's best friends, two noblemen with the mania of betting. They always bet on anything. This time, the wager is on a very particular game: they want to test Lorenzo's ability to resist feelings, to confirm if their friend is really, as he claims, refractory to love. But when a single man, though convinced, finds himself under the spell of the island of Ischia with Angie Cepeda at his disposition, it is no surprise that all defensive barriers may collapse.

The setting is a villa of Zaro, a splendid resort in the town of Forio from which you can enjoy breathtaking views of the Ischitan landscape. Other episodes use locations distributed throughout the island. The film is one of the most recent episodes of the attempt to relaunch the island's image.

3.7.3 A footnote on sound. Ischia and songs.

There are images of reality that we can enjoy with a direct look, which appear under our eyes, not unlike those created by painting, photography, and cinema, of which we have talked so far. But there are also "acoustic images", as the linguists say (Saussure, 1967), sound shapes, language and sound architectures that sometimes have an expressive power not less than that of shapes, figures, and images. It is also in this that the imaginative force of words is revealed. Those who almost always talk about something, tell a reality of the world. Here, Ischia has also inspired the pen of many writers and poets, a subject that obviously goes beyond the boundaries of our research. And yet, in modern times, poetry and especially songs, have so often crossed, as we have seen, the world of cinema, that we feel their creative operation is deservingly worthy of at least a few details. This is what we want to do here, recalling, for example, in the words of Palliotto, that, even before the cinema, "the Neapolitan song has offered its contribution from the earliest times to the beauties of Ischia, its sea, sky, plants and women". Gaetano Amalfitano in 1909 and Luigi Molinari in 1916 cite several examples of popular songs recorded since 1800 in Ischia, in particular at Serrara Fontana.

The first true song dedicated to Ischia is called "Ischitana" whose authors are the poet Vincenzo Ciprie and musician Giuseppe Salzano. The song was renowned for its refrain: "Ccà, nu cielo, nu mare na rena-ccà, I always talk about you."

Another success had another song of the same title, but very different from the previous one, whose authors are: Cristoforo Letico and Ferdinando Rubino. Thanks to Rizzoli, in 1953 Ischia is praised by many, especially by Domenico Tintomanlio, in art Tito Manlio, who dedicates to Ischia the song "Ischia, words and music". The success was such that it was continuously transmitted over the radio, and the Ischitans thought of returning the favour by dedicating a piece of land to him where he could have built a house. The great explosion of song creation took place in 1957 with Toto who composed "Ischia", Riccardo Pazzaglia and Domenico Modugno with "Ischia stands at mmiez o'mar", Nisa and Fanciulli with "Na house in Ischia", Hector de Mura and Mario de Angelis with "Green Island"; Vincenzo Acampora, Enrico Buonafede and Franco Colosimo with "Canzuncella to ddoie voce". At this point the ice between Ischia and the Neapolitan song had broken. In 1959 Stefano Canzio and Nino Oliviero write "love was born in Ischia". In the same year the restaurant was inaugurated: the "Rancio fellone" whose owner is Ugo Calise, a distinct singer known for his song: "Na voce, na chitarra, e o' poco e luna". Ischia was a privileged destination of all the famous celebrities of the time, such as Visconti, Tony Renis and all those who loved being in a worldly place "(Paliotti, 2002).

But the story was not over yet, in the late 1960s and early 1970s, the Neapolitan poet Pasquale Gallifuoco wrote, among other lyrics, a delicate song, "Ischia", which was brought to the forefront of the Neapolitan Song Festival from the late master Sergio Bruni. Song creation is a real tribute to the emotional and aesthetic sublime of the site. But the verses of the "green island" are above all a dreamlike image, "it is a shining dream that fascinates your heart." The poem interweaves fascinating metaphors that reveal the dimensions and aspects of the island's physical and sentimental landscape, authentic and sincere, that make us see them through realistic magic, like a panoramic terrace at sunset, or as in a precious movie sequence. Still, it is said that the Neapolitan poet, even though he is a man of the world, as it is said, had never visited the island and had never wanted to see it. For him perhaps Ischia was and must have a dream. His reality, however gorgeous, would certainly disappoint him. The island of his poetry was an imaginary Ischia, a place of the soul, an island of fantasy, an island that is not there and could not be there.

3.8 The Supermarket Island

As we have seen in the phase we are investigating, the island has lent itself, above all, to the creation of cinematographic works of not very high aesthetic value, mainly "cassette" films, which are rarely recognized for some particular expressive value. In the cases in which there is a trace of such value, this trait is attributed more to the impressive settings and to the quality of "photography" linked to the scenarios that the island has offered, rather than to the sophistication of the narrative solutions.

In fact, in the '70s, the general situation of cinematography in Italy is partly projected towards the disengagement of production, perhaps also in relation to the escalation of social conflict, the accentuation of labor struggles, the aggravation of the energy crisis, and the tragedy of terrorism which are, in short, among the factors that will profoundly mark the daily existence of Italians. In this context, while some important national authors are turning their attention to "committed" productions, such as those with very important social and political implications, another large sector of Italian cinema is directed towards evasion. That is, it is aimed at the creation of a copious production of B series films in which the accentuation of a vulgar, erotic side, at worst, and often beyond the worst of obscenity, could be seen as the attempt, however understandably appreciated by the people, of providing opportunities for "distraction" to an audience familiar with a difficult daily reality that doesn't lack elements of dramatic spectacle. It is obviously completely out of place to think about a manipulative project, consciously put in place to divert the collective attention from the real problems. It is more probable, instead, that the Italian film industry has grasped an understanding that in the "cultural" market there existed a real question of an evasive and light nature, and it equipped itself to provide a product that was able to effectively respond to this collective "imaginary need ". But, moreover, the success of the cinematic genre of pure entertainment is not only ascribable to the '70s.

Between cruises, trips to Egypt, Christmas holidays, Easter holidays, the break of Epiphany, school lessons, crews of sailors, carabinieri, firefighters, and among many others such as Boldi, De Sichi, Abbatantuoni, Izzi and the list goes on and on, the dominating wave of cinema has always found new performers and interested members of the audience. This it true up to the present day. In any case, it is certain that in the 70s the comic film genre, in the form of evasion, was widely diffused. It is also evident that Ischia has represented a special backdrop for this genre of film. Among the films worthily partaking in the stream of films made in Ischia during this period, we find **"La svergonata"** directed simply for the love of directing by Giuliano Biagetti in 1974. Stefano Amato starred next to a lascivious Barbara Bouchet in a film that tells of a series of casual amorous plots involving a family that arrived on the island of Ischia for the holidays. **Arrivano Giò e Margherito**, under the direction of

Giuseppe Coalizzi, is also of the year 1974. It is a fun comedy in which the two protagonists, Giò and Margherito, get into a series of predicaments in order to bring a mafia boss back to America. They are able to overcome their troubles thanks to the help of an impassive Englishman. The locals still remember the big street of Ischia Ponte adorned with numerous stands overflowing with tomatoes. Even the alley of Terra Zappata was transformed into a little market. The funniest anecdote is about the displeasure expressed by the local pharmacist who had to put up with habitual damages caused by a car that ended up off the road during type of car chase. An excellent representation of the group of licentious movies with Sicilian and Ischitan dapples is definitely the 1976 movie **La professoressa di scienze naturali** directed by Michele Tarantini which starred Lilli Carati and Alvaro Vitali. The plot is obviously very simple: a young supply teacher takes the place of a tenured teacher in a Sicilian high school. This young and recent graduate has a fresh and remarkable attractiveness that not only causes unrest at the school but also throughout the town. A plot along the same wavelength is **"La vergine, il toro e il capricorno"** produced in 1977 under the direction of the Italian producer, director and screenwriter Luciano Martino; it starred Edwige Fenech, Alberto Lionello and Alvaro Vitali. The movie is about a woman named Gioia who is so tired of her husband's continual infidelity that she decides to go to Ischia to betray him in turn. Her husband's pride was bruised and he seemed to have learned his lesson only until he gives in again, within a short time, to his penchant as a ladies' man. We move on to tear-jerker movies when examining the 1987 movie "Una tenera follia" that was directed by Ninì Grassia, a champion of poetry that is sentimental and of noteworthy

folkloristic characterization. He is also the director of the famous (at least on a Neapolitan scale) **"Cient'anne"**--like the song of the same name--that was filmed in Ischia in 1999. The main character is the late Neapolitan artist, Mario Merola, who as usual is involved in an actor-singer role. He is alongside a very young Gigi D'Alessio whose success at the national level was started thanks to this experience. In the movie, Gigi plays the role of Mario Merola's adoptive son, a promising singer. It is by chance that he discovers that the man for whom he is working is his biological father. In fact, this man is also the father of his rival in love: his biological brother, unbeknownst to him! This is a movie with strong melodramatic shades, with tears and songs that mix and mingle against the backdrop of "the green island". Even more recent is "**Se lo fai sono guai**", filmed in 2001 under the direction of Michele Tarantini. As an external set he uses the entire island; unfortunately, few are aware fo this movie because it has not yet been distributed. This makes one reflect on the fact that perhaps other movies have used beautiful views of Ischia and have never been distributed or perhaps they haven't highlighted the scenery's role in the movie and therefore it remains anonymous. In February 2008 (Cf., Coscia, 2008) there was news that shooting for the movie *Isola dell'amore*--the new blockbuster of the Vanzina brothers starring the unforgettable Anna Falchi and Aida Yespica, as well as Biagio Izzo, Ezio Greggio and
 Lino Banfi--would begin soon on various external sets, amongst which Ischia was included, naturally. They want to evoke the Italian comedy films of the 1960s. The show must go on.

CHAPTER IV: The take-off begins. Industrialists and intellectuals: an identical love.

4.1 The strategies of innovation

The second post-war period was an era of difficult rebirth for Italy. All the more so for an island like Ischia that was suffering from underdevelopment which dated back to the unity of Italy. The evidence of innovation, which had also been expressed, had a partial and episodic character. The island territory was still substantially characterized by conditions of extreme social and economic hardship (Mennella, 1999, p.23).

Among the fundamental options through which it was attempted, at this stage, to begin relaunching the island, was its insertion into the general framework of the programs for the economic and social development of the South (Cf., Saraceno, 2005). The six centers of the island, after a brief phase of unification, became independent municipalities, but all tried not to neglect the common goal: to give a new impetus to the economy.

With the war, the conditions of life of the islanders were aggravated. It was also for this reason that the migratory flow picked up again, as in many other parts, above all, in the south (Cf., Piselli, 1981; Pugliese, 2002). The destinations chosen by many Ischitan migrants at the beginning of the century were French Africa and France but in the second half of the 1940s were mainly the United States and South America, Argentina, Brazil. But several other islanders also chose Australia and Canada, which in those years saw a conspicuous influx of Ischitani (Di Meglio, 2001, p. 106-107).

Clearly, this phenomenon did not affect the whole island in a homogeneous way, but the internal municipalities were affected the most, those that were almost exclusively dependent on an agricultural economy based solely on the cultivation of the vine. But with the downy mildew and other problems deriving from the lack of intrusion of more advanced technologies (see, Cafagna, 1989), viticulture had been reduced to a simple family subsistence activity from the primary source of wealth that it had once been. The era of the revival and full exploitation of Ischitan wine would have come many years later.

At that time the situation was not the best not only in the rural areas of the island, for in spite of having very important tourist resources, such as the spas, they were unable to enhance them and use them as launching pads for the total take-off of their economic system. There were many unresolved problems in this area. Thermalism and vacationing were limited to short periods of the year and to circumscribed areas of the territory. The connections with the mainland were inadequate and insufficient, the roads of communication inside the island itself were too precarious as they had not received the necessary improvements; in fact, some of the old paths had been abandoned and were practically inaccessible. Being unable to fulfill the island's water needs was a serious problem due to the lack of submarine pipelines capable of bringing drinking water, of which the island is deprived, from the mainland. The procurement took place then through tank-ships, but in a discontinuous way. In addition, the supply of electricity was inadequate and intermittent.

But this condition of semi-underdevelopment, of wildness, a source of serious discomfort for the natives, appeared in the eyes of others as the image of a "natural" territory, an uncontaminated place, a space of primitive harmony of a world that now the modern era had definitely lost. Paradoxically, this allowed Ischia to become a destination for well-known personalities, men of culture, artists, thinkers, looking for an "oasis-shelter" where their considerable economic resources allowed them to live comfortably anyway. From the point of view of Ischia's "civil society", being aware of the degradation in the territory made it work in every way possible to find suitable solutions to establish a change. For example, young intellectuals from the area profused their energies to give life to different civic movements, also taking advantage of the experience of some members of the "Study Center on the island of Ischia", formed by a group of scholars of various disciplines; these initiatives helped to increase public hopes in the possibility of change.

The State had already established "l'EVI" in 1939, a specific institution for the development of the island, whose administration was interested in the entire territory of Ischia. This institution, in addition to the functions of an independent care and stay company of Ischia and Casamicciola, had larger tasks such as enhancing the entire area, building the streets, solving the problem of drinking water, completing the electricity grid, giving regularity to the implementation of the territorial plans.

For over ten years, due to the war, the activity of the EVI was limited and suffered serious obstacles. Despite everything, the landscape plan and the Calzabini plan were approved in 1943; the study of the potable use of local springs, a general local strategic plan of the island, unfortunately went missing (Castagna, 1990, p 63). A first step for a serious development plan was the convention organized by the Civic Committee at the Pio Monte della Misericordia in Casamicciola. The professor, Vincenzo Mennella, recalls that after the list of all the problems to be faced and solved the creation of a bridge that connected the island to the mainland was suggested—a hypothesis that today appears quite imaginative. Of course, the bridge was never built, but a series of much more significant "connections" were implemented: a large water pipeline, which still connects the island to the mainland, a series of submarine cables that allow electricity to arrive from the continent to the island and ferries that allow vehicles, for the transport of goods and passengers, to disembark and embark for the island. (See Mennella, 1999)

A description which helps us to better understand the island and its precarious conditions in the 50s is given by an envoy of the "Resto del Carlino" which in August 1954 describes it as follows: "Ischia ought not be included in the obvious span of contents of the Neapolitan landscape, so proclaimed, so poster-worthy (...) Ischia, on the other hand, shows a harsher tone: the pierced walls of the Aragonese Castle which appear to be falling, the vineyards of a champagne-yellow grape and on dusty land on which barefoot, beautiful and miserable children dart away, the cellars dug into the hills and closed by vertical rusty gates in cuts of bare ground, similar to the badlands of the Apennines, then there's the wine of Mount Epomeo that is accessible with mules and with donkeys, which is something primordial, picaresque "(Maldini, 1954).

Fortunately, some innovations, even if they were slowly affirmed, were realized, mainly thanks to the intervention of the Cassa per il Mezzogiorno and to the subsidized loans (Cf. Trigilia, 1994). Among the most important initiatives was the activation of the first cable for the supply of electricity, in June of

1951, which allowed the island to be lit up permanently for the first time. It was a great event even if after only four years the rapid development of tourism already caused energy saturation. The transport of electricity facilitated by the cable quickly proved to be insufficient, so much so that in 1957 it became necessary to design a second transmission system. This too quickly became saturated for the same reasons, thereby causing the need for periodic adjustment interventions which continued up to today. The projects continued with the construction of the submarine aqueduct built between 1952 and 1958. The water supplies, of small quantities and irregularly distributed, initially came from local sources, from tankers with large tanks, which received supplies from the mainland via lorries in order to fill the depots that were lacking water.

The arrival of the water was celebrated in the square of Ischia Ponte with a jet of water over 40 meters high.

Even the educational structures began to spread more and with them education on the island; at the professional hotel institute, the classes specializing in tourism and introductory accounting began. These areas of specialization at the level of higher education allowed young people a wider choice of training which, in addition to enhancing the level of know-how of the younger generation, also had an effect on cultural evolution with respect to the traditional image of the matrix of familism (Cf. Banfield, 1976; Putnam, 1993) which is considered typically widespread in the south.

The wine-vine culture also tried to recover: thanks to the interest demonstrated by Mario D'Ambra, adviser of the EVI, for the wines of Ischia produced in its six municipalities, the acronym D.O.C. "Denomination of controlled origin" and the adjective "classic" were recognized for wines of older origins produced in certain areas such as Forio, Lacco Ameno, Serrara Fontana and Barano. The event was celebrated by the islanders with a big harvest festival that consisted of many carnival floats and grape bunches which paraded in Ischia Ponte and made their way to Ischia Porto's bar "Bikini" for the conclusion of the event.

Between 1956 and 1960 infrastructures were built to facilitate connections between the different areas of the island thanks to state funding and the constant involvement of the EVI. In the late 1960s, the opening of the road to Citara gave way to the inception of the first thermal spa that could carry out outdoor healing therapies-- the POSEIDON gardens. After the opening of the Poseidon gardens, the creation of new thermal spas in different areas of the island soon followed: the gardens of Aphrodite Apollon di Sant'Angelo, the Castiglioni on the border between Ischia and Casamicciola, as well as many other private spas built inside the hotels (Cf., Delizia, 2001).

In this context a system of faster connections to the mainland could not be lacking. In short, alongside the considerable increase in the prospect of consumption by the middle class (not necessarily Italian), (see, Ragone, 1974), the situation on the island also improved with a certain speed, allowing for the accomodation of a large number of tourists who, in turn, they increased the economic resources available on the territory, thereby creating the conditions for further growth of the island's economy. This can be clearly seen by looking at the statistics related to the tourist movement (Cf., Volpe, 2004) which reveal how the number of tourists in the decade from the 1960s to the 1970s had undergone an increase of about 14% per year. In particular, we can see how the tourist flow was characterized by a noticeable increase in foreign tourists, compared to the national ones, in the period from 1963 to 1969.

We can certainly imagine how the increase in the number of tourists coming from other countries has been produced, thanks to the considerable circulation of promotional material, and, not of lesser importance, "word of mouth", especially in Germany. Whatever the case, the data on the extent of foreign tourist flow in those years speak very clear.

Table No. 1.

YEAR ITALIANS	FOREIGNERS
1963 63 %	37%
1966 58%	42%
1969 34%	66%

The economic and social changes that modernization has brought among the islanders can also be highlighted through data on the movement of the active population from one sector to another, as Felicia La Monica highlighted in her book: "Nel ventre della balena bianca". In 1936, out of 10.024 workers 54.4% were employed in farming and fishing. Instead, 15.2% instead found employment in the craft industry and in the construction sector, 24.4% worked in the service sector; from the post-war period to the seventies, agriculture lost workers with a shift from 52.4% in 1951, to 30.5% in 1961, to finally reach 10.4% in 1973. Simultaneously there is growth in the percentage of various jobs -42% in

1961 increases to 64.5% in 1973 (La Monica, 2002, p 31).

The tertiary sector evidently had a notable increase in many workers coming from families of peasant origin who moved towards jobs in the service industry. The sector grew thanks to the numerous opportunities produced mainly in the tourism sector due to the fact that it allowed one to earn more and to escape heavy agricultural work. Hotels and restaurants gave immediate employment to many people, especially young people, even if limited to the summer season. Throughout the rest of the year many sought work in Europe, Germany and Switzerland, above all. Those who lacked appropriate skill and experience remained on the island and got involved in the construction sector, almost always working illegally. (La Monica 2002)

On the other hand, the workforce of low levels of professionalism were necessary because of the economic boom which launched such jobs, as was the case in several other areas of the south, a movement of characters and results which still today are controversial (see Bagnasco, 1977; Caramiello, 1996; 2005; Saraceno, 2005). In short, it was a period of construction of numerous public works, roads, plants, and building renovations. Private individuals also built hotels and various facilities that contributed to the development of the tourism industry. Unfortunately, all this activity was counterbalanced by unbridled construction speculation which caused considerable damage to the environment and certainly contributed to the lack of any city planning regulations and any initiative for the protection of natural resources and the landscape. The magazine "Lettere da Ischia" originated in this period, a publication representing a moment of "critical" reflection on the distortions producing a process of modernization that is too accelerated and wild. Between its pages peeps out a light sense of nostalgia for past days. This periodical, managed by Giacomo Deuringer and taken over by the EVI, tried to rediscover places, traditions, popular and peasant culture, all of which are now almost forgotten. Unfortunately, since the magazine's efforts were made at the same time as the islanders' "chase toward wealth", the magazine's voice remained quite isolated and did not succeed in affecting the flux of the island.

4.1.1 The dilemmas of modernization: identity and nostalgia.

Indeed, the "conservative" memory of the "Letters from Ischia" contains sensitivity which in some respects is not lacking in "reasons". This memory has been evoked several times in different forms in successive eras, even in the context of the most recent era. Many of the fans of "Letters from Ischia" have not willingly accepted the transformations that the island is experiencing. Proof of this are some of the many testimonies collected by Raffaele Castagna "Ischia is no longer the island of the past – say some – it is now a metropolis. It seems at times that one is in one of the central streets of our mainland cities when the so-called rush hour strikes on the clock of all who are victims of the neuroses of modern life: buses, cars, car horns, gas clouds—all overbearing. There are also some characteristics that no longer exist in the cities of continent, such as the hysteria of the engines of scooters that have transformed into three-wheeled taxis... ".

Nowadays, according to some, Ischia no longer has a clear identity, but it is a hybrid, "a varied continent where the silent countryside is contrasted by the elite hotels and beaches, where mules climbing on the Epomeo are contrasted by the roaring three-wheeled taxis and where the lights of the fishermen are contrasted by the gigantic yachts of the Milanese ... ".

Even the spirit of the island seems altered, "everyone works in the tourism industry. Manpower costs one eye. Fishermen have become "rare birds". The fish come from the fish farms of Pozzuoli, from the Adriatic or from the most distant seas. Except for some praiseworthy exceptions, even craftsmanship is disappearing and with it so is the history of the island's traditions; it is said that in a home where there was craftsmanship the family members shared a special bond. A new tendency to assume common taste for products instead of unique ones creates a collective monotony that even for tourism is counterproductive. Nobody cares to increase the number of technical workshops or to bring back the art shops--which are prehistoric antiques-- in order to bring back appreciation for wrought iron, terracotta, embossed work, embroidery, wood carvings, handicrafts, all activities which basically stimulate the imagination of the working class. These deficiencies deny the masses of the opportunity to raise its evolutionary level. Every activity is exclusively for hedonistic speculation "(Castagna, 1990).

In conclusion, it is clear how on one hand, according to the opinion of various scholars, innovation has allowed Ischia to become a "product" capable of generating a wide tourist demand for the services it is able to offer. On the other hand, modernity ensured that Ischia lost its value and identity, thereby losing some of its admirers and enthusiasts, for example, travellers of a certain reputation such as Auden, who abandoned it in the early 1950s to move to a quieter place (Cf., Delizia, 2001).

In other words, also in relation to the size of the transformations suffered by the island territory and its community, several authors have called into question the issues related to the defence of identity. The fact is that this category, as Pecchinenda (1999) has shown, evokes a dynamic reality, a process, a becoming, and it is improper to use it as a dialectic tool to support people who hold on to the past or to support nostalgic positions, prejudicially adverse to progress and innovation (Cf., Caramiello, 1995, pp. 113-115).

4.2 Underdevelopment and Arcadia. Visconti's poetry and Rizzoli's plans

It was in this socio-economic context that the feeling between Ischia and the big screen was born, but it was not a mechanism based purely on random or spontaneous elements. For the establishment of this essential link between the cultural industry and the territory some "interventions" of great personalities, external to the island world, were the decisive ones, carrying different sensibilities and attitudes. We must, in this sense, think above all of the poetic wit of an artist such as Luchino Visconti and the aptitude as accomplisher and planner of a cultural entrepreneur like Angelo Rizzoli. Today we would not be able to imagine the transformation of the island of Ischia without the substantial contribution of these two icons of the world of entertainment and publishing.

These two personalities, engaged on different fronts in the Italian cinema in the post-war years, share in common their frequent visits to the island and their unconditional love for this place, traits which in many ways are contradictory to the reasons for which two major awards are linked to their memory: the "Rizzoli for the young Italian cinema" and the "Visconti". (See, Caprara, 2002, p 8)

The substantial difference between these two personalities was the conception of the island in its essence.

For Visconti, the almost "raw" expression of the territory and inhabitants, its manifestation at an almost primitive, uncontaminated stage due to primitivism and poverty--characteristics of the island of those years--was extraordinarily similar to an "ancient", primordial backdrop and for this very reason was a source of inspiration. He chose this setting for the expression of his art, so that he could elaborate his poetry of reality.

For Rizzoli, on the other hand, he had broad entrepreneurial designs--this poverty was not "poetic", it was a limit to be overcome, for himself and for those he met along his path. Perhaps this way of interpreting things also came from his personal memory. He had worked all his life to realize his own personal plans for freedom. He had never forgotten the hardship that he experienced because of his own modest origins, a childhood and a youth interwoven with personal suffering and destitution. This is why his desire was to bring development and well-being to the island.

We begin by telling the feelings that probably led the great Italian director to fall in love with a place like the island of Ischia, and that made him feel a love so strong for it that he wanted to stay there forever, wishing to be buried at the "Colombaia".

4.3 The Island of Il Gattopardo: Luchino Visconti

As it happens, basically, in relation to the "feeling" of every man we will never know, in an exact and unequivocal way, the nature of the feelings and of the thoughts that the island has unleashed in the soul of Luchino Visconti. Probably when the director was in Ischia, he felt he was recalled to a dimension of life, to an anthropological reality, which he thought had disappeared forever. The world of fishermen, the slow times of the peasant culture, the ancient gestures of its people, and the rock, the sea, the sunsets. A slow and silent community which offered him the physical and mental space that are ideal for his creative activity. Now, after many years, we can say that between Visconti and the island there was a real and very intense exchange. The emotional opportunities, the stimuli, and perhaps the opportunities for growth--on the intellectual and above all aesthetic level--were all given to him by the island and he has reciprocated such gifts, thereby structuring a cultural heritage, a material and expressive artistic heritage, 4.3 The Gattopardo Island: Luchino Visconti

As it happens, basically, in relation to the "feeling" of every man, we will never know, in an exact and unequivocal way, the nature of the feelings, of the thoughts that the island has unleashed in the soul of Luchino Visconti. Probably the director at Ischia felt he was recalled to a dimension of life, to an anthropological reality, which he thought had disappeared forever. The world of fishermen, the slow times of the peasant culture, the ancient gestures of its people, and the rock, the sea, the sunsets. A slow and silent community, which offered him the physical and mental space, ideal for his creative activity. Now, after many years, we can say: between Visconti and the island there was a real exchange, moreover very intense. The emotional opportunities, the stimuli, perhaps the opportunities for growth, on the intellectual and above all aesthetic level, that the island gave him, he has reciprocated widely, structuring a cultural heritage, a material and expressive artistic heritage of which all of us today are beneficiaries.

In fact, a man like Visconti, a forerunner of a new culture, a wide-ranging international, yet national-popular, a protagonist of the show, lover of detail, refined and engaging, fascinated by opposites and contradictions, could not remain indifferent to the enchantment of the island in the 1940s.

An island lived as a refuge, an escape, a surviving corner of authenticity, where the passage of time is still dictated by the ancient wisdom of fishermen and peasants--this was the idea of the great master of Italian neorealism, who imagined the island as the "quintessence of existence", "a place where the fascination of travel is found and the challenge to penetrate the mystery of things without having to spoil the "enchantment" (Castagna, 2001, p 35).

So, the first time that the great master came to Ischia - remembers Massimo Ielasi - he stayed at the hotel "Regina Palace" of the Pilato family. At this time his grandchildren were able to socialize with the islanders and discovered there was a possibility of renting " La Casarella " in Punta Mulino which in the 1940s was composed of two beautiful houses belonging to the Colucci family. It is right there that Visconti began to meet his guests and write some of his screenplays.

At that time the town of Ischia was becoming a pole of attraction for the world of cinema which eventually moved to the municipality of Forio. They were destinations sought not only by directors, but also by poets, writers, painters. A place to remember is *Bar internazionale* in Forio, a meeting place for many intellectuals who appreciated simple and sincere conversation with a genuine and passionate woman like Signora Maria Senese.

In 1948 the historian Nino D'Ambra described Ischia as "an island of peasant civilization and contracts stipulated with a handshake. A poor island full of needs "(...)" one of the most depressing places in Italy where infant mortality is still high. People, mortified by the war, do not appear to have given up". From this description one can imagine how the director was also a strong inspiration. During that period Visconti had been for a while in Sicily, to complete *La terra trema*, a film based on *I Malavoglia* by Verga. In the literary work, as in the film, the historical, economic and social reasons for the "Southern Issue" are gathered through a strong, naturalistic approach. The director seems to feel the need to observe closely, to become a "participant observer", to live from within or at least in close proximity to the traits of southern discomfort and to the historical and intimate "reasons" for this discomfort. In Ischia he finds familiarity with this type of reality, a social and anthropological context of which he has treated for a long time in his work. But the island, in addition to being a source of intellectual inspiration, was also imagined by him simply as a "serene" wild place in which there is not only the possibility to rest but also to live intense experiences in contact with nature; after all, given his eccentric personality, he could not love the "ordinary" quiet places. When years later he bought the villa "La Colombaia", located in the forest of the small town of Zaro, in Forio, he certainly did so because he considered it a place of quiet, but also of restless nature.

His friend and screenwriter, Suso Cecchi d'Amico, in an interview with Lora Del Monte, asserted when speaking of the "Colombaia": " (...) Luchino liked it very much and decided to buy it. He seduced the owners, who did not really want to sell it to him, but then they were persuaded by the passion that Luchino had for this house. He had the house completely redone with the help of all of his friends because he was an extraordinary host. It was pleasant being there, the house was really beautiful "(...) There was not even electric light (...) in the evening on a table by the entrance there were oil lamps ready and we went to the room with those (...) we went there to work, we wrote scripts there in the summer. The entire script for "Sense" was born there. I remember that we spent the afternoons doing spa treatments and in the evening we all had distorted faces (...). (Del Monte, 2001)

Although many considered him to be a very authoritarian, detached, austere person, (D'Amico, 2001, p 13) he became a close friend of some islanders with whom he established a deep and lasting relationship. This was the case with Jolanda D'Ambra, whose relationship intensifies to such an extent that the director defines himself as her brother. Likewise, is the relationship with Tonino Baiocco, another islander with whom he was very close. Here is his testimony.

"A lot has been said about Luchino Visconti, even by people who did not know him at all, but I can only tell you that he was a wonderful person. If he considered you a friend, he was extremely open and affectionate. He was a very reserved man, a man of great raffinity, always kind in his ways. A great character. When he entered the bar, he obviously aroused the attention of everyone, but to him that interest made him almost embarrassed. To give you the exact idea of how Visconti was made, I can tell you a very small anecdote ... One day, a friend of mine, she calls me and tells me, Tonino but do you know that you are mentioned in a book by Visconti? I did not know anything about it, it was a book I owned, but I had not read it. I realized, to my amazement, that Visconti actually mentioned me in the book, but he had never told me about it. Basically, he was not one of those people who do something to make an impression or to get attention because it would be talked about. He was in no way an exhibitionist. He did things and that was it, discreetly, because he felt like doing them. Here is the book, "Vaghe stelle dell'orsa", it is from 1965, a life has passed, Visconti talks about the film, about his cultural passions, about his idea of cinema. It was published by the publisher Cappelli, and here is the part where I am quoted. At that time, I took off with my Alfa Romeo for Volterra to bring to him the perimeter measurements of the Colombaia that he was having built. Helmut Steniberger came with me-- he later became a great actor with the name of Helmut Berger--but then he was just a boy who stayed at the "Garden", a hotel in Ischia Porto. We had become friends because he used to drink at night at the "Lampara". He was a beautiful boy who attended the hotel institute in Lausanne and had come on vacation on the island. Since he became very close to me, he wanted to accompany me to Volterra to Luchino's place. He did not come with me because he heard of Visconti and wanted to make films-- he was a boy who did not need anything and was from an excellent family. In short, we left together and the next evening we arrived in Volterra.

We found it difficult to find accommodations and ended up in a house that Visconti had bought in the area and was putting in place, an old monastery. And it was there that Luchino and Helmut first met. Helmut Berger was created from that encounter ... I introduced him to Visconti ... Helmut met him there

... and so began the story of Helmut Berger. Not his artistic career ... because before making him star in a film Visconti really made him work his way up the ladder... Visconti moulded him, made him study, he turned him into an artist, it's not that he found him there already set and ready ". Tonino Baiocco was the owner of "La Lampara", the hub of the island's nightlife, in which Visconti was a regular guest with all his dear friends such as Suso Cecchi D'Amico, Enrico Medioli, Paolo Stoppa, Rina Morelli, Franco Zeffirelli and many others.

Visconti probably saw in his friend a reflection of himself as a young man, the same restlessness, the same stubbornness, the same ambition. The bond was so strong that Visconti served as Baiocco's best man at his wedding and Baiocco's first child was named after him. This is the period in which the director feels he is approaching old age, he is less and less worldly, and he goes out more and more rarely (Cf., Castagna, 2001).

Given his love for the island and his skill as a director, one may spontaneously ask why his love was never expressed in some cinematographic work, and why Visconti never filmed in Ischia or about Ischia? Responding to these questions is Salvatore D'Ambra, a historical figure from Ischia, heir to the world famous D'Ambra winery. His answer, apparently simplistic, contains complex reasons. "The first years were fun and entertaining and the director could not bear that the set would be a place of entertainment, but it was supposed to be a place where maximum professionalism reigned of the highest rigor. Later, when other directors chose the island as a set, Visconti pursued a very personal idea of cinema; he considered himself totally free to follow the inclinations of his taste, of his sensibility".

If any ideas were there, they inevitably arrived after the maximum time limit. And yet, towards the end of the 1950s, Visconti attempted to set up a theatrical performance on the Aragonese Castle; he spoke about it with his closest friends and collaborators and requested the necessary permits from the municipal administration led by Vincenzo Telese.

The answer was however negative; an unpleasant veto prevented the tie of Visconti with the island of Ischia to be made official by means of an artistic consecration. "It was a huge pain for him, he became very angry," says Salvatore D'Ambra, who realized that behind that veto there was "the will to punish his never hidden sexual preferences." He could not bear that the prestige and esteem that he enjoyed everywhere were disintegrated by the hypocritical prudence of some politician invaded by sacred censorious fury. "(Castagna, 2001).

But in spite of everything, he became attached to the island so much that he wished to be deposed in this place so as to remain there forever; in this way he gifted the island with an artistic and material legacy from which all the islanders benefit. (Martorelli, 2001) So, as per his will, as of August 11, 2003, his ashes and those of his sister Uberta are finally placed right in the precise spot indicated by him in the Colombaia garden: behind the house, gazing over the sea along the bay of San Montano. Moreover, always as per his will, the twenty-fifth anniversary of his death coincided with an important event for the community of Forio: the villa's opening to the public, which, in the meantime, has become home to an international school of Cinema and Theater. With this free gift from Visconti Forio has become a cultural reference point of European importance.

In 2006, a year that commemorates the centenary of his birth, besides being the headquarters of the

Visconti Prize, placed under the High Patronage of the President of the Republic, it has also become the heart of international celebrations in honour of the director.

4.4 Rizzoli's plans

The story of the great protagonists of the history of cinema, linked to the green island, would be told in a hasty and partial way-- indeed in a literally incomplete manner-- if we did not refer to the splendid and profitable relationship that Commendatore Rizzoli developed with island and its inhabitants over the course of decades. Between the 50s and 60s, the municipality of Lacco Ameno became a place of research and study, not only thanks to the discovery of important archaeological remains (Castagna, 1990, p26) but also for the innovations made by Angelo Rizzoli. According to the legend, everything seems to have originated from a phone call that Prof. Malcovati, trusted gynecologist of Rizzoli's wife and daughter, one day telephoned the commendatore to ask him to set up an appointment to talk to him about a very "urgent" matter (Morgera, 2002, p.13). Rizzoli was very frightened, he thought of the worst, he thought that the thing that Malcovati had to talk to him about was the health of his women. But his terrible concerns were immediately dispelled when he met with the doctor. Malcovati only wanted to ask him for a loan of 100 million to set up a business able to exploit the healing benefits that he believed the area's thermal waters possessed. Rizzoli sensed a good deal and together with other doctors founded the business: "Pithecusa", to enhance the island's thermalism. For reasons which Malcovati did not share, he had no way to repay the loan, and then sold his block of shares to Rizzoli.

Rizzoli ended up with total control over the "Pithecusa" business and was convinced that the spas had to be next to an elegant hotel. He bought from the Capasso family he bought the structure on which would later rise the "Regina Isabella". He also founded the business "Incremento Isola d'Ischia" which bought the Terme Manzi di Casamicciola. Shortly thereafter he put the two businesses together and created the "Ischia Terme Spa" (Morgera, 2002, p.14).

But Rizzoli's interest was not limited to Lacco and Casamicciola; the industrialist was serious about enhancing the whole island, equipping every Ischitan municipality with a high-level spa. But these plans of his were also destined to encounter serious obstacles. The administration of the town of Ischia Porto, for example, did not consider leaving too much room to work with, almost imposing on him the intervention of Count Marzotto in this project of his. However, Rizzoli and Marzotto came to an agreement with a sort of "gentleman's agreement" in which Marzotto would promote the hotels on the island and Rizzoli the thermal baths. Count Marzotto violated the agreement by creating an elegant thermal property within the Jolly hotel (located in the municipality of Ischia) with funding received from the Cassa del Mezzogiorno. For Rizzoli, the Count's casual manner, backed by the local administration, was cause for serious disappointment. He was immediately insulted and decided to invest only in the municipality of Lacco Ameno, even without funding from the Cassa del Mezzogiorno. Unfortunately, the political choices of those years which were aimed at limiting Rizzoli's initiatives ended up hindering the economy of the entire island, for Rizzoli had also change the name of the business to *Lacco Ameno Terme*.

Between 1960 and 1966, Rizzoli added to his vast empire the hotels "Il Fungo" and "le terme del Capitello", he expanded the "Regina Isabella", the "Royal Sporting" property was created and inaugurated by Gina Lollobrigida, and he modified the "Villa Svizzera" property. Thanks to these operations, the volume of business that in the 1960s exceeded one billion reached a total value of 2.3 billion over ten years. It should be noted that the island economy was moving upwards, the Rizzoli companies employed about 450 workers, 90 in the spas and more than 300 in hotels. At the "Regina Isabella" there were more than 200 employees who rotated in various ways their responsibilities for 130 beds. "The ratio was 1.5 employees per customer. An employee of the spas in 1955 could earn 60 or 70 thousand lire a month, but the level of the guests was such that some of them, like the engineer Astaldi or as a certain Adriano Olivettti from Ivrea, left tips of 50 thousand lire "(Morgera, 2002, p 20-21). Functional to his logic of development in 1962, the first hospital of the island was inaugurated by the commendatore who dedicated it to his wife, calling the hospital "Anna Rizzoli". But he did not stop here. Angelo Rizzoli, elected honorary citizen of Lacco Ameno, also took an interest in the spa of the "Reginella"; at that time he "brought to life" the Cinema "Reginella" (today's Congress Center) in which he projected previews of the films of his Cineriz media company. (Mennella, 1999).

He was a businessman, evidently, an entrepreneur with a strong practical sense, one who rightly looked after the profit, but no one can deny that he did everything in his power to improve the island. One should know that he even transferred his residence to Lacco Ameno, making his "family tax", which rose to about eighteen million lire per year, flow into the cash registers of the Municipality as the municipality faced difficult financial conditions. It should be noted that during these years the entire incidence of the family tax, in Lacco Ameno, amounted to about twenty million, so all the rest of the population contributed only two million. (Mennella, 1999, p 37-38).

4.5 The passion of a self-made man.

Today the Rizzoli dynasty continues under the direction of Angelo Rizzoli Jr., the grandson of the legendary commendatore, who has linked his name to the green island. But, beyond the anecdotes, what were the most profound reasons that led his grandfather to make investments in Ischia? The grandson, Angelo Rizzoli Jr., has his own answer and he also formulates hypotheses. Here is his testimony. We need to know one thing, and it is that the commendatore, "the first time he went to Ischia he arrived from Capri and could see the extraordinary difference between the two islands: the same beauty, although diverse, contrasted with the extraordinary wealth of Capri compared to the equally extraordinary poverty of Ischia. It struck him that two islands that were hardly far from each other were treated so differently: Capri was a luxurious center of the international elite, while Ischia was experiencing a great state of neglect.
This inequality struck a chord with my grandfather whose philosophy of life was founded on the very poor childhood that he had experienced; over the years he had nourished himself with socialist ideas, and consequently, having made a lot of money, he felt the need to commit to assist the working class. In fact, he did not only concern himself with Ischia; he built several hospitals, the new Martinitt house in

Milan, and the Marzabotto paper mills to make up for the massacre that this martyred city suffered during World War 2. I think he must have said to himself: "I am a Milanese industrialist who made money in the north; a part of this money is reinvested in the poorest, most unfortunate Mezzogiorno, to give the people of Ischia an opportunity for work and wellbeing, especially in tourism "(Caprara, 2002, p24-25).

Angelo Rizzoli does not only hold a spot in Ischia's collective consciousness, for he will also always be remembered as the man who was raised in an orphanage as a poor and needy child and was able to get to the helm of publishing, cinematographic and hotel empires that are among the largest in Europe. (Morgera, 2002, p 7)

He himself talked with pride about the poverty he lived with as a child: "We lived in misery in a very rich area of Milan. It's the worst thing there is, believe me, to be poor among the rich. I remember that the happiest day of my life as a child was February 10, 1895, when I entered the male orphanage known as the Martinitt. There I was finally happy because I was a poor person among the poor, one like all the others." (Occhipinti, 2000, p 96). In fact, as a symbol of his past, on display as a keepsake and coat of arms in the atrium of his modern establishment in Civitavecchia is his first linotype which he bought with the savings of his earnings as a typographer. Typography was the trade taught in the Martinitt orphanage, and it seemed as if there was still in him a piece of the worker that he used to be .....at least it seemed so just by the way he greeted people by bringing his hand to the visor of an imaginary tray instead of that of a hat. (Montanelli, 2000, p 81-82).

Although Rizzoli was not a man of culture, he knew how to handle business deals perfectly. A significant description of Rizzoli's work is that given by Indro Montanelli: "Of the prose he put under the press he knew nothing. But of the men who came to offer it to him, he did not let himself be bedazzled. A glance was enough for him to weigh them to the milligram. People said he had the touch of King Midas, the gift of turning everything he touched into gold. (...) I also saw an application of this "touch" on the day he decided to produce "La dolce vita". Fellini was not yet the sacred monster back then that he deservedly became. And of the plot of that film that was without plot, as he told it, it was clear that it would cost an eye from the head. When I asked why he had taken over the enterprise, Rizzoli replied: "Because that guy there ... what's his name? ... if he can make others act as he acts, he will certainly do something that maybe does not sell, but that was worth doing ... "(...) He had understood the value of Fellini a few years before everyone else." (Montanelli, 2000, p 84-87).

And nobody like him at the time understood the importance of supporting Ischia in the world in the different ways possible: with tourism investments, through his periodicals and with the business activity of his Cineriz media production company. Thanks to his contributions, Lacco Ameno became a meeting point for VIPs, royal families, Hollywood actors, industrialists, show business and culture celebrities, but it became above all a centre of the Italian film industry, a must for many stars of the Italian and international cinema, for right in Ischia they played various roles in different films. An example was Charlie Chaplin, the famous Charlot, who chose to present in Ischia, in the cinema Reginella, the opening night of his not unforgettable work, "A King in New York".

In Lacco Ameno's theatre the great masterpieces of Cineriz were shown, as well as famous American films. Lacco Ameno became terrain for comparison between the expressive research in the national field, which was not without high moments, and Hollywood cinema. Residents and tourists, at the price of 500-600 liras, could witness the debut of highly worshipped films of that time period. (Morgera, 2002, p 54)

Among the celebrities that were close to Rizzoli, in the cinematographic context, and with whom he had a less formal relationship, we should mention: Gigetto De Santis, who took care of the press office, the screenwriter Leo Benvenuti, who signed some very important works and the producer Peppino Amato, with whom he founded the "Riama". But there were also several others who were among the most valiant directors and actors of the period and who had regular contact with Rizzoli. In fact, it was from his encounter with Fellini that movies like "La dolce vita", "Giulietta degli spiriti" and "Eight and a half", winner of the Oscar for best foreign film, arose (Morgera, 2002, p 55).

Great success was also achieved with the series "Don Camillo and Peppone", a series of films-- taken from the stories of Giovanni Guareschi-- which enormously fascinated the working-class public as well as others in the 50s, and literally won easily at the box office. It was also thanks to the proceeds of those cash ins that the construction of the Albergo della Regina Isabella was started.

The cinematic success of Cineriz reserved for him, among the many awards, also many famous prizes: in addition to the Oscar for the movie "8 1 / 2", there was also "Il biglietto d'oro", "Il nastro d'argento", "La palme d'or of the Cannes festival ", "Il David di Donatello ", just to name a few. The continuous

presence in the world of cinematography offered him the opportunity to meet and frequent fascinating women, among many of his favourites were: Miriam Bru, Graziella Granata and Isa Miranda. But beyond these particular "friendships", the commendatore considered the places where Anna Rizzoli lived sacrosanct and never used them for his affairs...
further proof of the fact that he shared a deep bond with his wife.

4.5.1 The commendatore in the pen of the great ones

A bizarre, unpredictable and controversial celebrity, he solicited the curiosity of the most important observers of the Italian scene after World War II. Writers and journalists wanted to meet him and get to know him to discover the secrets of this multifaceted and many-sided celebrity.

He remained in the memory of Oriana Fallaci as: "A person who was baffling, unthinkable, unique, a mosaic of incongruities, a labyrinth of possibilities. He was a factory of creativity "(Fallaci, 2000, p 69).

Many, like Gaetano Afeltra, say that he knew how to pursue his interests as a great entrepreneur with cunning, determination and even crudity; but he was also able to manifest enormous sympathy, spontaneity and gratitude towards his collaborators (Afeltra, 2000, p 13).

It is said that before the second world war, he already possessed a billion, and that at his death, in 1970, the heirs found one hundred in cash. He was not proud of it, he said that "one must be forgiven for having money", and that everything was more expensive for him (Biagi, 2000, p 60).

Michele Prisco always remembers him dressed in white, with a fake yellow and white plastic cigarette that smelled of menthol and that hung from the corner of his lips. He remembers that Rizzoli did not forgive him for writing a book in which the protagonist women died one after the other: it was the novel "Gli eredi del vento" with which he won the Venice prize for an original work, and which according to the competition announcement was to be published by Rizzoli's publishing house. It was as of that time that their relationship began. After some time had passed Rizzoli confessed to Prisco: "Do you know that Clouzot was interested in your novel and would like to make a movie? I told him: dear sir, a film in which the actresses die one after the other will not get a penny, it's pointless." Thus, Prisco lost an opportunity and took it with philosophy (Cf., Prisco, 2000).

This man left an indelible mark on the mind of those who knew him, for he gave a little of himself to everyone, whether one was famous or down-to-earth. And it is from his humble beginnings that he drew the characteristics that made him fascinating, of great sensitivity for society and of an honest simplicity in his manner (Andreotti, 2000, p 35).

4.5.2 A trusted technician: stories told by a foreman.

The head maintenance technician Gabriele, now blind, worked for Angelo Rizzoli for a whole 40 years, following him also in the various business activities that the commendatore had in progress in Milan. When he talks about his employer, Gabriele is still moved today. He describes him as "the greatest man that ever came to Ischia"; a man who looked to the future, a great entrepreneur who did not only think about making money, but also looked after the well-being of his employees. For them he even "built three six-story buildings, A-B-C each one with an elevator".

His love for the island was such that in his large office in Milan, in front of his desk he had hung a huge picture that covered the whole wall, a painting depicting the entire town of Lacco Ameno with the mushroom and the "Regina Isabella" hotel.

"I still remember the esteem Rizzoli felt for me and the words he would use to introduce me still seem to echo: 'Ischia, (so he called me), is an honest man, with a sense of work and family, (...) these are the men I have in Ischia .. (..)' he'd always say". Gabriele remembers that when the commendatore had some plans for the island, his ideas were not aimed at a reality to be exploited only for business purposes, but at a place that he felt belonged to him intimately. Once in Milan, precisely in Canzo, Rizzoli told him: "We have to bring these paintings and this furniture to

"our land". In fact, the Meridiana that is now located outside the Regina Isabella hotel was dismantled from Milan and reassembled in Ischia". Gabriele does not see us but his mind is clear as he pulls out one memory after another; it is like an overflowing river.

"Once he stopped to look at a large painting with a huge horse head and he observed it looking very distracted. I thought he wasn't feeling well but instead, after a while, he called me and putting his hand on my shoulder said: "I have built an empire from nothing and maybe my children will destroy it." In order to reveal the type of soul that this man possessed and how he related to the simple people, Gabriele narrates that one day on the main street of Lacco Ameno, near the tobacco shop, he was watching the elderly chat along the seashore and said to him: " 'How they are nice these old men, they are happier than me' and while he said this, I heard someone call out to me: "Gabe, where are you going?" Rizzoli understood Neapolitan well, and I replied "I'm going for a walk" and he addressed the commendatore by saying: "Ange, don't you remember me, I am Vespoli, we saw each other so many times in Naples". He paused to reflect a moment, then embraced and kissed the man, saying "Vespoli, I thank you. You reminded me of the good times ", then took 1000 lire and said to me: "Give your grandfather some cigars". It was not an isolated incident, for in Ischia he gave money to anyone who approached him, but he did not want to be taken advantage of otherwise he wouldn't give anything away. During the Christmas holidays--he did not want this to be known-- he gave each Martinitt a huge package. He had many plans for Ischia, but he was not permitted to realize them. He wanted to invest in Sant'Angelo and make it a tourist centre all year long, (...) he also bought a large plot of land at the Maronti that was not accessible, not even on foot, and he had the mule track built. This mule track was a beautiful road that could be traversed on foot or with the mule, for Rizzoli had plans made to make this a tourist centre. His dream was to bottle the water of Nitrodi, (...) In Lacco Ameno, in order to make the heliport we had to use tons of land which we shovelled from the area where the hospital was being built. He also wanted to make a large heliport in Forio, but it was not permitted (...). For the Lacco Hospital he bought and installed the best equipment, but nobody knew how to use it".

Gabriele also remembers the interest that Rizzoli had for the inhabitants of the island: "When the spa was opened, he began to hire affable young men and women, he had trades and professions be taught to them by expert teachers who came from outside of the island--masseurs, doctors, beauticians--and the islanders had to learn. The same was true for the hotel, the best experts in the field took care of the training of staff: cooks, waiters, sommeliers had to undergo a professional apprenticeship. For the commendatore guests were sacred, for they brought wealth and therefore had to be treated well, with care and respect, and had to find serenity and cordiality at the spa, in the hotel ".

Since the girls of Lacco Ameno were in contact with the hotel's clientele of splendor, they began to dress better and were fashionable. After all, for at least a few months of the year in many families the salary of several hotel staff members would come through which allowed a lot of people of Lacco Ameno a good standard of life. But the old Gabriele has some recollections also of the relationships that the commendatore maintained with the people of the world of cinema, "he was very close to Walter Chiari, who also his son's godfather. He also had a great relationship with Mario Camerini; just think that at Villa Arbusto, there was there was a separate house which Rizzoli made available to him every time he came to Ischia. He was an extraordinary man, who enjoyed the esteem and consideration of other exceptional people. The testimony of Gabriele is completely consistent with the things that are usually heard in Ischia by anyone, even those who have never met Rizzoli. We can certainly affirm that few men have succeeded in winning the spot in the hearts of the Ischitans that the commendatore occupies. And today, a long time since his death, there is still great esteem and affection for Rizzoli on the island and not only in Ischia. His is one of those adventures, an American one if you will, the "difficult" story of a simple and practical man who, starting from nothing, managed to achieve great goals, merging his aspirations as an entrepreneur with the needs for progress of his country.

CAP 5: The new presence of cinema in Ischia

5.1 The spotlights come back on

After the golden years of the innovative venture of the film industry's presence on the island, a time when so many people gravitated chaotically toward the orbit of this peculiar fragment of an industry that was placing importance on culture, today the scenario has become quite transformed. There are no longer individual celebrities who are spontaneously motivated in the sector; if on the one hand today the situation has lost a certain fervour, compared to past years, as it scales itself down due to economic influences and the changing intensity of the phenomenon, on the other hand it has been enriched by a certain professionalism.

Currently on the island there is a special agency to take care of locations and cine-television casting: "The Ischia Film Agency".

Michelangelo Messina, its creator, is a man who has always had a strong passion for cinema and who has worked in various ways to preserve his historical memory on the island. The collective memory of the innovative age and of the "golden years" understandably tends to fade with the succession of generations and succeeds, with difficulty, in imprinting itself in the minds of the youngest. The organization which Messina has set up, in addition to being a logistic structure, in addition to helping the directors with their filming, also provides information on how to obtain images of the most characteristic places and contributes to the making of films while providing all kinds of cultural and technical support for film and television productions. After having a tradition that we have witnessed as being solidly rooted in the field of film production, the island has become an interesting scenario even for television products.

The first TV series which took place in Ischia was "Il Commissario Raimondi". Created in 1998, its protagonists are Marco Columbro, Barbara De Rossi and it is directed by Paolo Costella.

Perhaps it was also thanks to the attention garnered through television that soon afterward the world of cinema regained interest, in various ways, in the island context. Not only did Mario Merola shoot "Cient'anne" there, but the island also hosted the filming of a thriller like "The Talented Mr. Ripley", based on a book by the famous Patricia Higsmith, which was then followed in 2001 by the production of "Se lo fai sono guai ". 2003 is the year of the production of the film directed and performed by Leonardo Pieraccioni: "Il paradiso all'improvviso". Pieraccioni, for the first time during his career as a director, shoots a film in the south. For Ischia it is a great advertising opportunity at the national level. Obviously, it is a film to be placed, in perfect continuity, after those respectable national-popular comedies, as it is a vehicle of that effective cine-tourism that was "invented" by Rizzoli many years before. For the island, in short, it is a "mega postcard" sent from as many as ten locations distributed over the six municipalities of which Pithecusa is composed.

Also, in 2003, for fans of the soap opera "Un posto al sole", Ischia became a delightful location for some episodes: Forio, with the beautiful scenery of the church of Soccorso, and the "Bagno Antonio" of Ischia Porto, places preferred by the screenwriters as settings for shooting.

Obviously, as was the case in the past, the presence of extras was necessary. Whenever there was a call for extras, many came forward, eager to be chosen.

Of course, today's reasons for auditioning as an extra are very different from those of the past. What motivates one to desire a role as an extra is no longer poverty, as it once was, but the pleasure of being exhibited, of showing oneself, of "emerging", of being noticed on the big screen. There is the hope of possibly obtaining a "role" in one's own small way, in the hope of getting a job as a showgirl on "Striscia la Notizia", or to take the place of the unfortunate Taricone in "Big Brother".

In any case, in 2006 the island is again in the camera lens. "42 plus" is an Austrian production directed by Sabine Delfinger. The story is quite classic. There is a woman in her forties, or rather of "42 and +" years old, who arrives on the island for a vacation. It is an opportunity for her to come to terms with her adulthood, with his dissatisfactions, with her regrets. And it is also an opportunity for encounters. The woman is still beautiful and charming and she is not willing to live the rest of her life by simply cherishing memories; it is not surprising that she captures the attention of a handsome blond boy who makes her feel deeply alive again. The passion that overwhelms them is capable of offering deep and intense emotions, but it is also a trigger for a profound predicament which not only damages the balance and dynamics of their relationship but it also reveals fears and anxieties. The film has a beautiful picture which is revealed not only in the interior of the splendid Ischitan villa where it was filmed, but also in the trolley shots, in the subjective shots with an island backdrop and in the various sequences that compose it. The views on the ferry, the beach of Cava, the promenade of Casamicciola, the folkloristic illuminations of the popular festival of Forio, are the setting for this story with a strong existential connotation. **Andrea Sarnelli**, director of the

"Italian Location" in Naples, oversaw the logistics of the film, during the phase of its realization in Ischia. Let's hear his story. "In three weeks, all the interiors had been filmed - says the manager - at the beginning there were only two planned external locations, given that the film was shot almost exclusively in this beautiful villa. Then as the island was visited it was discovered that there were so many other places that could work. The director was passionate and we ended up with 12 external locations. We shot in all six municipalities. Although we ended up disturbing virtually all of the island of Ischia, the mayors were happy and welcoming. We filmed at Cava, Sant'Angelo, Forio, Negombo and in many other places. It is clear that the island always has magic and suits cinematographic endeavours. As for images, the resources for them are immense, starting with the narrow streets which retain their traditional character because of their somewhat ancient style from Magna Graecia, and the most modern structures which also have a remarkable charm. You can mix a promenade, a typical Mediterranean coastal strip, with an almost mountainous hinterland, which, moreover, also reaches a considerable height. There are landscapes that have a South American feel and some perspectives that make you feel as if you are in Hawaii. In this film we have deliberately respected the local setting, even with an implicitly promotional cut. We went to shoot in the various municipalities, also taking the road signs with all the names of the localities and geographical indications. Every square, every street is clearly visible. We even kept the original name of the restaurant in Ischia Ponte: "Ciro e Caterina". I must also say that we have found much friendliness and kindness everywhere: truly a beautiful calling card. You know, when you become part of the atmosphere of the island you also feel a bit like a son, as happened to those who were part of the production. They were completely taken in by the local atmosphere. I wouldn't have thought so before, but I discovered that the Austrians, where character is concerned, also have something Neapolitan inside them. "

In 2009, Ischia was chosen as the location for the television series "**I delitti del cuoco**" with the participation of the legendary Bud Spencer in the guise of a former commissioner who would like to enjoy old age by opening a restaurant in Ischia.

Nine years later it is followed by "**L'amica geniale**" that features Ischia, Naples and Marcianise as the locations of an Italian-American television production created and directed by Saverio Costanzo. The series is a film adaptation of the first book in the series of works published by an unknown author who became famous internationally under the pseudonym of Elena Ferrante. It must be said that it was in Ischia that a crucial and painful sequence was shot based on a scene in the novel that reflected the protagonist girl's development as an adolescent. The series is publicized under the title of *My Brilliant Friend* in anglophone countries.

L'amica geniale, a bestseller published in 2011, has sold over seven million copies. It is the first volume of the four-volume literary series of the same name. The other three novels are: *Storia del nuovo cognome* (2012), *Storia di chi fugge e di chi resta* (2013), *Storia della bambina perduta* (2014).

The narrative scene of the film, faithful to the structure of the book, is populated by a crowd of characters who make extensive use of acting in dialect. The narrative scene develops in various environments reconstructed with cinematographic rigor and recalls the customs and characteristics of a people and of an era: the discomforts and the real misery of the post-war period and the slow and difficult transition towards a modest lifestyle within a context in which the charm and the dangers deriving from the presence of the underworld is always felt. The series is performed in the Neapolitan dialect.

5.2 Epomeo: Ciak is filmed.

Filmmaking in Ischia also is a lively cultural reality made up of moments of encounters, promotional events, national and international exhibitions; it is an activity that has borne fruit since the early 1960s.
In 1962, among the events promoted by the EVI and those carried out by the various municipalities and associations, a special place is occupied by the "*Epomeo Ciak*" and the "*Epomeo d'oro* ". This last initiative, however, was directed to the music world. The "Epomeo Ciak", had a consistent echo because it represented the initiative that closed, every year, the period of the great international film festivals.
In reality, it was an opportunity to celebrate Italian cinema, a trend that has established itself in the world for its artistic quality and its ability to intercept popular taste. The award had its own two reasons for existing. On the one hand, it valued the first authors of the successes of cinematography: actors, directors, producers, scriptwriters, technicians, critics. On the other hand, it served to publicly express the gratitude that the Island of Ischia had towards the world of cinema, a means of great promotional capacity for the island because of the numerous works which were realized on the island and then diffused throughout the world. The objective was to reward not the films of recent production but the highest figures in the international world of cinematography. The award ceremony took place in the "Reginella"

cinema of Lacco Ameno, always in the presence of an exceptional public (...) In the 1963 edition, the "Epomeo Ciak" badge of honour was given to the knight of the event, Sir Angelo Rizzoli, in recognition of his fruitful work as a film producer. Along with the knight commander, there were cinema personalities who were also given awards: Catherine Spaak, Paulette Goddard, Cesare Zavattini, Mario Monicelli, Eduardo Spadaro, Sandra Milo, Antonella Lualdi, Enrico Maria Salerno, Steve Reeves, Monica Vitti, Vittorio Gasmann, Rossamo Brazzi (Cf., Castagna, 1990). In 1972 the Angelo Rizzoli prize for screenwriters was also established, an award which for many years had great cultural significance and aroused considerable interest.

5.3 Festivals return to Ischia

The tradition of the great film festivals regained popularity in 2003 with the genesis of two important initiatives: the "*Foreign Film Festival*" and "*The Ischia Global Music & Film Festival*".
The two festivals are both of important significance. The Foreign Film Festival addresses, in order of significance, the appreciation of the locations, the relaunching of views of the landscape, settings and panoramas of Italy (without minimizing the importance of those of Ischia), in an attempt to relaunch Italian film at the center of international film production.
On the other hand, the Ischia Global Music & Film Festival focuses its attention on aesthetic and technological innovation, with particular reference to the relationship between the Italian film tradition and new emerging innovations in cinematography at the international level. The interest of the first edition

was significant because it concerned the digital format as well as Indian film production, the so-called "Bollywood" cinema.

5.4 The Foreign Film Festival

Although for many years the "Angelo Rizzoli" film award has been absent, the "Foreign Film Festival", conceived by Michelangelo Messina, tries to give the island the same artistic and cultural value expressed in the past. The idea of the festival, considered an event of excellence for helping to revive tourism, was shared by many experts in the world of cinema and aroused widespread media interest. This media interest is useful for drawing attention to the aspects of cinema that are usually taken for granted but are instead its beating heart: the locations.
With the festival, the desire was to promote familiarity with Italian landscapes, especially those of the Italian islands, and to encourage national and foreign productions to choose our country as an ideal set for shooting films. The award is an artistic recognition for those who have chosen less familiar locations and who have promoted them for tourism and culture, thanks to shooting movies there. Movies are free promotional vehicles—there are many examples to support this theory. Let's consider Tuscany: the whole world got to know of Arezzo thanks to Roberto Benigni's "La vita è bella" which was honoured even in Hollywood. The Benedictine monastery of Sant'Anna in Camprena will always be remembered as the set of Anthony Minghella's film "The English Patient" (1966) while San Giminiano is known thanks to Franco Zeffirelli's "Un tè con Mussolini" (1977). Last, but not least, Ischia was put in the spotlight thanks to "The Talented Mr. Ripley" and the island of Procida became known to the world

thanks to Massimo Troisi's "Il Postino". These movies have intrigued and fascinated viewers to the point of positively influencing them to choose our country as a holiday destination.

On the other hand, the process of internationalization of Italian cinema is indispensable for its very survival. In order to make this process a reality, the national industry must be of a magnitude that suitable for competition. Without giving up the so-called "commercial films" which in a productive and rich market fuel the industry, the same industry which allows for the creation of "artistic films". France and Germany have understood well that filmmaking contributes in a crucial way to the promotion of the local culture and that the landscape and settings can assume importance that is not inferior to that of a star. Michelangelo Messina, the host of the **Foreign Film Festival,** has a very clear idea about this matter; it is very closely tied to the meaning of the event that he promoted. Here are some excerpts from his testimony that have been entrusted to the world of telecommunications: "The Foreign Film Festival" is a festival dedicated to a well-defined theme, that is to say, the relationship that exists between cinema and land and has the clear goal of systematically linking these two entities: in fact, cinema and the places in which its stories are realized have always walked side by side but without dialoguing coherently. We are the first and unique festival in the world that has a contest and awards for film-TV productions that have either greatly promoted the land or have expressed the land's culture. But we also have another goal. We would like to be able to ensure that new producers in connection with a specific area would invest in co-marketing operations. It is a matter of creating the conditions under which the production of the film or the TV series will find the advantageous economic conditions in a given area and then choose to film. For its part, that area receives an immediate economic return (hospitality of the crew, use of local companies and workers, etc.) and of medium term, all thanks to the remarkable inner workings of advertising which is always connected to the production of works of this kind and to the possibility of becoming part of the movie tours network, that is to say tourist stays in places where films and TV series take place.

Of these synergies there are already successful examples, especially in the Anglo-Saxon countries, the United States (remember those dedicated to very successful TV series such as The Sopranos and Sex and the City in the USA), New Zealand, where the colossal "The Lord of the Rings" was filmed, Great Britain, where there are over 100 locations for films based on the "Harry Potter" saga.

 Our festival wants to be a moment of contact and comparison between the experts of this sector, therefore, from the producers, to the set designers and scriptwriters because the co-marketing projects begin already in the film's scriptwriting phase. Messina is convinced of the importance of this orientation, also in relation to the consequences that certain cinematographic strategies can have on the tourist economy of the areas in the field of cinema. "Seeing a film can amount to a journey, an emotional and cultural journey but it can also become properly geographical because we tend to go in search of the places that we have discovered and they have struck us thanks to having viewed a particular film ". Messina is strongly convinced of the importance of cinema for the purposes of tourist development of an area. Unfortunately he complains that in Italy, in this land, we are very far behind: "although scattered throughout the country there are 1500 locations used by cinema and TV: but to insert a certain number in a network of movie tours it takes organization and also a historical memory, while also taking into account that different regions do not even know the cinematographic cultural baggage that belongs to their land.

From studies promoted by us in collaboration with the BIT of Milan, it emerged that for decades the sampled countries, namely Germany, Switzerland, France, Sweden, chose Italy as a holiday destination because of its portrayal as a carefree country as seen in "La Dolce Vita". In the last 20 years this situation has changed: an emblematic example is the strongly negative impression of Sicily mediated by products like La Piovra. With the series of Inspector Montalbano which celebrates a positive Sicilian character, this trend has had an inversion. Apart from that, Italy is still promoted by films which are widespread at the international level: the old American epics such as "The Godfather", Fellini's films, international films such as "Ocean 12" but also "Life is Beautiful" by Benigni". Even though he lays claim to the authenticity and autonomy of the initiative that he set up, Messina recognizes the value of the other event that takes place on the island, "Ischia Global", without even excluding the possibility that their paths can converge in the future: "We both move into the world of cinema, but our festival is dedicated to a specific theme, while the other one is dedicated to cinema's evolution, to news, with international guests but have chosen not to have a film competition. The Global Film Fest is a great event that has the opportunity to dialogue with the celebrities of cinema and brings them to the island-- this constitutes a beautiful advertising showcase for Ischia. We are much more technical, but one festival does not exclude the other. We have distinct identities, but we are talking about attempting to unite because as the only European entity dedicated to film tourism, together (thanks to Ischia Global's parterre of guests) we could become much stronger and compete with national festivals such as those in Venice, Rome and others elsewhere ".

5.5 Ischia Global & Music Film Festival

The Ischia "Global fest" wants to establish an occasion of high interest and appreciation towards the Italian film tradition and cinematographic art in general. The inaugural edition took place in Ischia, in the Lacco Ameno area, in the summer of 2003 and continues year after year.
In an enchanting natural setting, outdoors, with a maxi screen of 20 meters mounted on a large stage, with the sea in front to act as the backdrop and scenography, the setting, created by the Carriero family, was a worthy setting for the return of cinema and culture to Lacco Ameno. The initiative attempted to tie again the threads of memories of a remote past of splendor. But today, with many efforts, with unquestionable tenacity and determination, there are those who try to project that memory into the present. It was seen at the initiative's opening night. Prestigious guests, that is, personalities of culture, art, and politics, crowded a prestigious parterre and inaugurated the Festival space at the Regina Isabella in front of one of the most evocative views of the island of Ischia and the entire country.
Among the prominent figures present were: the actor and director Kabir Bedi of the popular television series Sandokan of the 70s who is today a star of Indian cinema that has conquered the world; Jean Claude Van Damme, one of the most beloved actors in the world, who welcomed on the spectacular stage

the prestigious previews and accompanied the international superstars, guests of the event, while also presenting the preview of his film "The Hell". In addition, there were Stefania Sandrelli, a legend of Italian cinema and beauty, the director Peter Greenaway, F. Murrey Abraham, Ornella Vanoni, Nicola Carraro, Biagio Agnes, Anna Falchi, Eleonora Brigliadori, Gabriella Carlucci, Luis Horvitz one of the most prolific Hollywood film directors, Marina Cicogna, Marcello Veneziani, Ida Di Benedetto, Philippe Martinez and others. It seemed as if the times of the legendary knight commander, Angelo Rizzoli, had returned.

When called to the stage, each of the stars lavished words of love for cinema and admiration for an island which is too often far from the spotlight and is instead placed in a shadow cone where it certainly does not deserve to stay. The most unexpected convergence was between Nicola Carraro and Peter Greenaway who were at odds where business interests are concerned. Both ended up evoking, like a soul whose presence benignly hovered over everyone, the figure of Angelo Rizzoli. The words of his nephew recalled what anyone familiar with his story knows well: the commendatore had two great loves: Ischia and the cinema. He confessed to me, in fact, in a nice chat at the bar of Queen Isabella, that his grandfather "was more of a patron than a producer, he had made money, of course, but he kept intact the desire to dream and pursue his dreams". With the same spirit, the first edition of the conference "Ischia Global Film & Music Fest" began. In terms of cultural content, the initiative marked, since its debut, the dual needs to which it is directed. On the one hand, the need to adapt to technological innovations, starting from the evolution of the digital system as an epochal turning point for cinema and beyond; and on the other hand, to focus on the new position that Italian cinematography assumes in relation, from time to time, to those of other countries, especially "emerging" economic and cultural realities. The first festival was dedicated, as has been said, to Bollywood.

A great deal of space was dedicated to the promotion of Indian production films, but at the same time to researching the most appropriate strategies to make the reverse phenomenon possible (that is to say, bringing Italian films to other countries and giving them the same importance). According to the promoters of the initiative, the line to follow can only be that of inserting Italian cinema in a stronger context: the European one. Hence the idea, which the festival pursues programmatically and I would even say "institutionally", of making various types of agreements with the institutions of other countries to ensure that Italian cinema can be more and better distributed. An example of this would be implementing an effective co-distribution policy, which means bringing Italian cinema, first and foremost, into the European context, making the business and cultural dimensions usefully dialogue and interact while preserving the specific character of individual cinematographic traditions. Not surprisingly, one of the distinctive features of the Festival is, at each edition, the organization of a conference, a discussion between experts and operators that acts as a bridge, to intensify the exchange of relationships, between anthropological universes, identities, cultures. The discussion and the comparison between different experiences represents, in the spirit of "Ischia Global Film", an important opportunity, to know, analyze and debate common production problems in the global society.

All this is always accompanied by special screenings, meetings and comparisons on the hottest themes of cinematography which are followed by splendid gala evenings. The venture, being at every edition a real cultural full immersion, has already produced visibly significant results not only recognized by industry and communication professionals. It has certainly made inroads among the sector's opinion makers, its image has been relaunched by the international press, consolidating the role of Ischia as one of the most important and prestigious centers in the field of culture and entertainment.

In the wake of all of this, a Prize for young film talent (*Premio per i giovani talenti del cinema*) was created, an award dedicated to the memory of the young Isabella Rizzoli, thirteen years after her tragic death. The young twenty-three-year-old woman known as Andrea and Lyuba Rizzoli's daughter, took her life on 19 July 1987. The mother Lyuba Rizzoli and her godmother Marina Cicogna, wanted to remember her in the first edition of the Festival by tangibly helping two young future artists, two girls who showed great talent and ability together with an extraordinary passion for cinema. Two scholarships, worth 6,000 euros each, went, in fact, to the two most brilliant students of the National Film School (*Scuola Nazionale del Cinema*), chaired by Francesco Alberini and Caterina Cecchi D'Amico.

This venture is also aimed at the goal of bringing Ischia back to the world capitals of cinema, music and culture as in the days of the legendary producer Angelo Rizzoli. In short, it is a question of relaunching an image and an overall organization of the island on a cultural and social level, capable of giving new impetus to its development.

More specifically, this development is the growth and evolution of this very important component of the southern Italian territory whose economic expansion can be considered an authentic factor of a more advanced social trait, but only if it will be accompanied by an identical momentum and progress on the civil and cultural terrain. The Festival's activity is closely intertwined with the initiatives that the Ischia International Art Academy has been carrying out since its foundation. The organization, chaired by the engineer Giancarlo Carriero, actively works in the field of promoting the image of the island through cinema and promoting the cinema through the image of the island. As we approach the final phase of our reasoning, it is appropriate to report the ideas with which the President Carriero illustrated the premises and the aims pursued by his organization. Below is his inaugural speech at the first edition of the Festival.

5.5.1 The testimony of the President of the Accademia Internazionale Arte-Ischia.

"The first time I had access to the Regina Isabella Hotel I was little more than a lively child. I was struck by the image of the sea water pool, a few meters from the cliff, the large number of waiters at the restaurant and the immense table of desserts of which I was fond. I was thrilled by the presence of Walter Chiari, the idol of the Saturday night broadcasts, while I fail to recall the presence of a celebrity who was staying with elegant discretion: Mrs. Audrey Hepburn, too refined to strike a teenager. "But how, don't you remember? At least in the piano bar ..." they keep asking me today. "Unfortunately, I do not", I keep repeating. I don't remember her also because the wonderful salons of the hotel were forbidden to us kids from sunset onwards. So ....

Someone who struck me immediately was also a gentleman who was not very tall, greeted by everyone, always smiling, who acted like a true master of the house: the knight commander Angelo Rizzoli, a name destined to be a legend. When my family took over the ownership of this wonderful facility two years ago, I sat for the first time in the armchair of the Regina Isabella Hotel, a chair which I suppose was used by the knight commander Angelo Rizzoli during his happy days in Ischia. After a few moments of sitting recklessly on that hot chair, I was pervaded by the feeling that I was about to assume an important responsibility in history and in the world of business procedures. I immediately had the perception that I was about to face the most demanding professional adventure I could imagine, but also the most stimulating. In fact, while caring for the facility and while admiring the sophistication of its details, I still felt the spirit of the years of my childhood and of the characters who contributed to making the name of Ischia legendary. I understood that that spirit, still intact, is the secret of the charm of the facility.

Reckless and passionate about challenges, together with my father Leonardo and my sisters we planned a series of investments to relaunch the services, organization and image of the Hotel with the intent of reliving the glories. In this context we also thought about a film festival, as in the tradition of Angelo Rizzoli, but before taking off with this we waited for the development of an original idea that combined cinema and music and that looked strongly to the future. An idea, refined by the brilliant friends gathered around the table of the non-profit association Accademia Internazionale Arte Ischia.

The idea aims to give Lacco Ameno the role of being the capital of the star system, but which simultaneously promotes reflections on technological innovations, on the relationship between cultures and ethnic groups, and on whatever else contributes daily to the transformation of international society, while respecting ancient values, especially memories. An event, therefore, that took into account the positive component of globalization. The spirit with which Angelo Rizzoli moved on the green island Angelo Rizzoli was modern, so the attitude with which we will face this fantastic new adventure with history will be equally modern so as to respect the path that the great knight commander has left us as a legacy".

CONCLUSIONS

The identity of a social context is always the result of a union, of a mixture, between what a space expresses in terms of orography, territory, physical habitat and what it represents in one's imagination.
In other words, a physical habitat is always and simultaneously a cognitive situation, a mental habitat. And these two dimensions always experience, in a gradual and constant, or simultaneous and sudden way, mutability, transformation, change. And every change that occurs in one of the two spheres is destined to have serious repercussions on the other, to condition its *evolution.* It is like saying that if the way one imagines a place changes for one reason or another, then the mechanism of transformation will inevitably ruin the material nature of the place, its organization, its meaning, its identity. This would be similar to a change in the structure of a territory that would end over more or less a long period of time and would cause transformations even in the way of being of the people. In other words, the perennial transitional nature that characterizes this relationship ensures that the identity of individuals and communities, like the nature of places, is only a fleeting episode of a transformation process condemned to never being interrupted. A social territory like that of the Island of Ischia has experienced, over the course of long historical periods, and in a violently accelerated way in the last decades, transformations of every kind which are, for love or by force, reverberated in the mentality of its inhabitants. Such transformations have produced changes of great importance which have profoundly changed the memory, the image, the character of the green island and its population. The island, as we have shown in various ways throughout

this work, has always been a junction of anthropological paths, a crossroads of worlds, stories, cultures.

Since ancient times it has been a preferred landmark for the creation of legends that have found a place for mooring and docking on the rocks of ancient Pithecusa. And yet, this place which is so strongly characterized in a historical, folkloric and symbolic sense, is to be looked at, in a more disenchanted way, like a territory that has experienced very difficult economic and social problems. Ischia was also, until a few decades ago, a social territory characterized by poverty (both material and symbolic), marginalization, and unmet needs. An island of sailors, of farmers, like all the islands of our South, for which the sea, rather than being a space inviting research, conquests, and adventures was configured as a barrier, an obstacle, a physical limit to the relationship with the Italian peninsula, with the continent, with the world.

It was this trait that made the island preserve until the dawn of modernity, its naturalness, its wildness, which has fascinated many artists, travelers, creative and ingenious men. And so, almost unconsciously, the island began its dialogue with the international imagination, and so its people have kept their reluctance, their distance from modernization, trying by every means to guard their unlikely arcadia.

Then something happens, it happens that a new, unpublished, unknown and fascinating device comes into play, definitively undermining every shyness, every reluctance, every distance. Ischia, can no longer keep away from modernization, speed, the market, fashions. The cinema bursts with the force of a hurricane over the ancient harmony of the community, breaks its traditions, brutalizes its value systems. The cinema arrives in Ischia, bringing with it the news of the world, its colors, its "show".

It's the 1930s, the troupes land on the coasts of Ischia to capture, in kilometers of celluloid, those locations finally discovered and destined to fascinate film-makers from all over the world. The "dream factory" is also an industry of reality; for the poor people of the island the money earned from film productions is perhaps the first important opportunity for liberation. For each one there is a small occasion, from the skilled carpenter to the peasant girl who will experience the thrill of appearing as an extra in some blockbuster, or in a boorish film cassette.

And so, Ischia begins to see its image spread throughout the world, it begins to attract tourists from all over, it becomes a preferred place, a land of sophisticated and still elite holidays. A few more years later Angelo Rizzoli will discover its beaches, its ravines, its warm and sulfurous waters, and will make it his home. With the advent of Rizzoli, the island definitively enters modernity. At this point in time, it's not just sophisticated (and perhaps a bit snobbish) intellectuals that love the island. And that wildness so appreciated by Luchino Visconti will soon become a memory. The island attracts travelers and vacationers, hosts awards and festivals, and this pushes other tourists to the island in an endless "virtuous" circle.

Its inhabitants have finally understood the business and now every small landlord is planning to become a hotelier, every modest cellar man is equipped to transform himself into a sophisticated restaurateur, and the humble potter has now achieved the best quality craftsmanship.

The economic boom, as we have shown in this work, witnesses the strengthening of the image of the island as a holiday industry. The 1970s witness the masses consecrate Ischia as a legendary place. What helps promote the island is always cinema which is more and more rarely "refined" and more and more usually "commercial". But business is still booming until the 1980s which witness signs of a certain decline and even some serious symptoms of decline. The years between the old and the new millennium see instead a certain revival of the charm and attractiveness of the island which returns to being recognized as a reference point for the international tourism industry. But the glories of the 1960s are definitely far gone. Today the island needs a new stimulus, an injection of confidence, a positive boost. We need to bring it back to the international stage (which has already started to be accessed by the island, according to some signs). Once again, we need to illuminate Ischia and put it on display. Perhaps it can be the cinema again to accentuate its image. The location has only changed a little, but the island still has much charm to express. In short, the set is ready and many directors are willing to set their stories on the green island. But who will be the Rizzoli of the third millennium?

Luigi Caramiello (1957) is a professor of Sociology of Art and Literature at the University of Naples "Federico II". He has taught at the University of Salerno, the University of Bologna, the Parthenope University of Naples, the University of Naples "L'Orientale", and at the University of Budapest. He has published 22 books and is the author of more than 400 scientific articles and papers. Luigi Caramiello is a professional journalist, critic, director for RAI, and is enrolled as an author in SIAE (the Italian Society of Authors and Editors). A member of UNAR (the Italian Office against Racial Discrimination) of the Presidency of the Council of Ministers, he has supervised various research projects and participated in numerous conferences and international ventures. Among his publications are the following: *Il medium nucleare*, Roma, 1987; *Da amore a Zapping*, Napoli, 1995; *La natura tecnologica*, Napoli, 1996; *L'ambiente della comunicazione*, Roma, 1998; *La droga della modernità*, Torino, 2003; *La gioventú del Silenzio*, Napoli, 2007; *Frontiere Culturali*, Napoli, 2012; *L'energia politica*, Napoli, 2015; *Percorsi di sociologia dell'arte*, Padova, 2015; *Il Maestro dei Grandi*, Brescia, 2016; *Oltre il luogocomunismo*, Napoli, 2016; *Sulle Strade della Musica*, Napoli, 2017; *L'apocalisse immaginaria*, Napoli, 2019.

Marianna Sasso (Ischia, 1976) graduated from the University of Naples "Federico II". From 2003 to 2006 she has completed research studies on the filmography and on the history of the Premio Cinematografico Angelo Rizzoli (the Angelo Rizzoli Film Award); these studies have been published in the anthology *Ischia e il Cinema* (Valentino Editore, 2008). She has worked together with the Department of Mental Health in Ischia's ASL Napoli 2 (Local Health Authority Napoli 2) to assist with the recovery and rehabilitation of troubled and at-risk individuals. Marianna Sasso is the author of the research article *"Impatto sulla depressione. Un osservatorio sui costi farmaceutici ad Ischia, in (a cura di Emilia Cece) "Le depressioni. Diagnosi, trattamento e prevenzione dal passaggio all'atto"*. She is currently living in Peterborough (UK) where she is teaching Italian.

Anna G. Di Meglio graduated from the University of Toronto with an Honours Bachelor of Arts, a Master of Arts and Bachelor of Education. She also obtained the Italian Professional Translation Certificate from the University of Toronto's Faculty of Continuing Studies. She has been enjoying teaching Modern Languages for over 20 years while leading an active lifestyle.

BIBLIOGRAPHIC REFERENCES

A.A.V.V., (a cura di), Centro di studi sull'isola d'Ischia, *Ricerche Contribut Memorie* Atti relativi al periodo 1944-1970, Amodio Napoli,1971

Abruzzese A., *Arte e pubblico nell'età del capitalismo*, Marsilio, Venezia, 1973.

Afeltra G., Com'era Angelo Rizzoli , in , *Angelo Rizzoli*, RCS; Milano-Roma, 2000

Algranati M., *Ischia vergine* Interlisano 1° edizione, Napoli, 1959

Andreotti G., "Aveva studiato soltanto alla scuola della vita, in *Angelo Rizzoli*, RCS, Milano Roma, 2000

Arias G., *La questione meridionale*, Zanichelli, Bologna, 1921.

Aristarco G., *"Cinema"* N° 27, 30 Novembre, 1949

Aristarco G.,	*L'utopia cinematografica* Sellerio editore, Palermo, \ 1984.
Armstrong R.,	Billy Wilder, American Film Realist, McFarland & Company, Inc. Publishers Jefferson, North Carolina and London, 2000.
Bagnasco A.,	*Le tre Italie*, Il Mulino, Bologna, 1977.
Balàzs B.,	*Il film. Evoluzione ed essenza di un'arte nuova*, Piccola biblioteca Einaudi, Torino, 1987
Balestriere G.,	*A Ischia cercando Luchino Visconti,* Imagaenaria, Ischia, 2004
Balestriere G.,	*Angelo Rizzoli Zio d'America d'Ischia*, Imagaenaria, Ischia 2005.
Banfield E.L.,	Le basi morali di una società arretrata, Il Mulino, Bologna, 1976.
Barbieri G.,	Il *villaggio di Sant'Angelo\ nell'isola d'Ischia,* le origini la storia-le tradizioni. Edizione Associazione\ culturale "C. Mennella", Forio, 1989

Barbieri G.;	*Ciak, si gira Ischia isola cinematografica* Ediz.ne Ass.ne Cult.le Cristoforo Mennella, 2004

Bassoli V.,	*Storia generale del cinema* Orsa Maggiore Editore, Torriana (EV),1987.

Bevilacqua P.,	*Storia della questione meridionale*, ESI, Roma, 1974.

Biagi E.,	"*La strada si chiamava Via Civitavecchia, in, Angelo Rizzoli*. 1889-1979 RCS; Milano Roma, 2000

Bianchi L.,	" *Candido"* 30 luglio 1950.

Braudel F.,	Il mediterraneo, Bompiani, Milano, 1987.

Brunetta G.P.,	*Cent'anni di cinema italiano* Editori Laterza, Bari, 1998

Buchener D.,	*L'isola d'Ischia* Studio geografico, Istituto di geografia dell'università di Napoli,1965

Buchner G., Rittman A.,	*Origine e passato dell'isola d'Ischia* G. Macchieroli editore, Napoli, 1948

Buchner P.,	*Ospite ad Ischia*

Imagaenaria, Ischia, 2002

Buford K., *Burt Lancaster an American Life*, Alfred A.Knopf, New York, 2000

Buonocore O., *Leggende isolane* 2° edizione, centro di studi sull'isola d'Ischia, Rispoli Editore, in Napoli, 1956

Cacciapuoti U., *Case d'Ischia* Edizioni d'Arte Pithecusa Ischia, 1961.

Cafagna L., Dualismo e sviluppo nella storia d'Italia, Marsilio, Venezia, 1989.

Campari R., *Il racconto del film* Generi personaggi immagini. Biblioteca di Cultura moderna Laterza 1 ediz., Bari, 1983.

Campbell J., Mito e modernità, RED, Milano, 2007.

Canetti E., *La provincia dell'uomo*, in opere 1932 –1937, Classici Bompiani, Milano, 1990

Canova G., *Le garzatine cinema* Garzanti, Torino, 2002

Caprara V., *Ischia e il cinema* Il tirso, Ischia, 2002

Caramiello L., *Da amore a Zapping*, Pironti, Napoli, 1995.

Caramiello L., *La natura tecnologica*, Curto Editore, Napoli, 1996.

Caramiello L., "*Le ragioni di una rivista*", in, Take Off, Esselibri, ottobre 2005.

Castagna D., (a cura di) *Un set colorato di verde e di azzurro,* Speciale Scuola, Bibliotheca Le Maree, Ischia, 2002.

Castagna G., "Luchino ed i suoi amici", in,Tonino della Vecchia, (a cura di) *Gli anni verdi. Luchino Visconti ad Ischia* Istituto italiano per gli studi filosofici, Napoli, 2001.

Castagna R., *Lacco Ameno e l'isola d'Ischia. Gli anni '50-'60 Angelo Rizzoli e lo sviluppo turistico* Cronache e immagini La rassegna d'Ischia, Ischia,1990

Chandler C., *Nobody's Perfect.Billy Wilder. A personal Biography,* Simon & Schuster, New York, 2002

Chiti R., Lancia E., *Dizionario del Cinema Italiano.*

	Film dal 1930 al 1944, Vol 1, Gremese Editore, Roma, 1993.
Chiti R., Poppi R.,	*Dizionario del Cinema Italiano*. I film dal 1945 al 1959, Vol 2, Gremese Editore, Roma, 1991.
Clinch, M.	*Burt Lancaster, Stein and Day*, Publishers, New York, 1986.
Coscia B.,	"*Bellezze da isola*", in, Corriere del Mezzogiorno, giovedì, 14 febbraio, 2008.
D'Ambra N.,	*La rabbia di Leopardi contro Napoli. Per Berkley, Standal e Croce, l'isola d'Ischia era terra di avidi selvaggi*, in, "*Ischia mondo*" n° 130, Maggio 1987, Ischia
D'Ambra N.,	*Eruzioni e terremoti nell'isola d'Ischia* Centro ricerche

	storiche D'Ambra, Forio d'Ischia, 1981
D'amico M.,	"Luchino", in, Tonino della Vecchia (a cura di) *Gli anni verdi. Luchino Visconti ad Ischia*, Istituto Italiano per gli Studi Filosofici, Napoli, 2001.
D'Antonio M.,	(a cura di) Lavoro e disoccupazione nel Mezzogiorno, Fondazione Agnelli, Torino, 1992.
D'Ascia G.,	*Storia dell'isola d'Ischia,* Li Causi editore s.a.s dalla Li.Pe. in San Giovanni in Persicelo, Bologna, Ottobre 1864.
De Juliis E.M.,	*Magna Grecia. L'Italia meridionale dalle origini leggendarie alla conquista romana*, Edipuglia, 1996.
Della Vecchia T.,	(a cura di) *Gli anni verdi. Luchino Visconti a Ischia*, Istituto Italiano

	per gli Studi Filosofici, Napoli, 2001.
Delizia I.,	"La terra trema!Dal cambiamento al caos", in, Tonino Della Vecchia (a cura di), *Gli anni verdi. Luchino Visconti a Ischia*, Istituto Italiano per gli Studi Filosofici, Napoli, 2001.
De Seta C.,	*L'Italia nello specchio del grand tour* In Annali della storia d'Italia, Vol V, IL paesaggio, Torino, Einaudi, 1982
Del Monte L.,	"Di un senso profondo. Colloquio con Suso Cecchi D'Amico", in, Tonino della Vecchia (a cura di) *Gli anni verdi. Luchino Visconti ad Ischia* Istituto italiano per gli studi filosofici, Napoli, 2001.

Deuringer G.,	L'Epomeo d'Oro, in *"Lettere da Ischia"* Rivista di vita turistica dell'isola d'Ischia Anno I, (serie nuova) N°2 Autunno 1963
Deuringer G.,	*La 'ndrezzata* I quaderni dell'isola verde, a cura dell'Ente Autonomo per la valorizzazione dell'isola d'Ischia Napoli,1957
Deuringer G.,	*Ischia. Guida turistica dell'Isola.* Napoli, 1959
Di Costanzo G.,	*Voci per Ischia* Da Boccaccio a Brodskij Imagaenaria, Ischia, 2000
Di Maio S.,	*Breve storia del regno di Napoli* Da Carlo di Borbone all'Unità D'Italia (1734-1860) Ed tascabili Newton 1986
Di Meglio B.,	"Tutti i film girati nell'isola d'Ischia", Serie di articoli pubblicati in Ischia Mondo, Numeri: 205;

	207; 208;210;211;212;214; 215;216;217; 218; 219;220;221;222;223; 224;225;226;227.
Di Meglio P.,	a) *Ischia natura, cultura e storia* Imagaenaria, Ischia, 2001
Di Meglio G.,	b) *Ischia ieri e oggi* Editoriale Albal s.a.s Ischia, 1987
Fallaci O.,	"Era un uomo di mille pudori"in, *Angelo Rizzoli*. 1889-1970, Milano - Roma, 2000
Freudiani G.,	*Ignazio Gardella e Ischia* Officina Edizioni, Pavona Albano Laziale, Febbraio 1991
Galasso G.,	*Il mezzogiorno nella storia d'Italia,* Le Monnier, Firenze, 1977.
Hillman J.,	*L'anima dei luoghi*. Conversazione con Carlo Truppi, Rizzoli, 2004.

Hirschmann A.O., *La strategia dello sviluppo*, La Nuova Italia, Firenze, 1968.

Hitchcook O'Connel P., and Bourzereau L., *Alma Hitchcock. The Woman Behind The Man*, Berkley Books, New York, 2003.

Iasolino G., *De rimedi naturali che sono nell'isola di Pithecusa, hoggi detta Ischia,* in Napoli Appresso Giuseppe Cacchy M.D.L.XXXVIII

Ielasi M., (a cura di), *Artisti dell'isola d'Ischia* Società editrice Napoletana, 1987

Kanè P., *Sur Avanti*, Cahier du cinema 248, September 1973 January 1974

La Monica F., *Nel ventre della balena bianca, società politica ad Ischia dal '46 al '76* Imagaenaria, Ischia, 2003

Lubrano A.,	*Il patriota L. Settembrini non è mai stato sul Castello d'Ischia*, in *"Ischia mondo"*, n° 1, Maggio 1987. Ischia
Malagoli E.,	*La tradizione culturale ed artisti dell'isola d'Ischia*, Istituto italiano per gli studi filosofici circolo G. Sadoul, La città del sole, Napoli, 1998
Malagoli E.,	in, Ielasi (a cura di), *Artisti dell'isola d'Ischia*, Società editrice Napoletana, 1987
Maldini S.,	"Cronaca su Ischia" in, Castagna (a cura di), *Lacco Ameno e l'Isola d'Ischia* Edizione La rassegna d'Ischia, Lacco Ameno, 1999.
Mancini E.,	*Flegree isole dei verdi vulcani* Natura, storia, arte, turismo di Ischia, Procida e Vivara Mursia, Milano, 1980
Mancusi L.,	*Dopo 80 anni di onorata attività i*

	Castagna chiudono col Cinematografo, in Ischia Mondo, n°143, Marzo 1989, p 15.
Martorelli A.,	"Una partie a Zero", in, *Gli anni verdi. LuchinoVisconti ad Ischia.* Istituto italiano per gli studi filosofici, Napoli, 2001.
Mattioli F.,	*Sociologia visuale* Nuova ERI, Torino, 1991
Mennella C.,	*Isola d'ischia Gemma climatica d'Italia,* ed E.D.A.R.T, Napoli,1958
Mennella V.,	*Lacco Ameno. Gli anni '40-'80 nel contesto politico amministrativo dell'isola d'Ischia,* (a cura di Giovanni Castagna) Edizione La rassegna d'ischia, Ischia, Gennaio 1999
Mereghetti P.,	*Il Mereghetti* Dizionario dei film 2002 Baldini & Castoldi, Milano, 2002

Meterangelo F.,	*L'isola d'Ischia. Guida turistica* Tommaso Marotta editore, Napoli, 1986
Metz C.,	*Semiologia del cinema* Garzanti, Bologna, 1972.
Minghella A.,	(edited by Timothy Bricknell) *Minghella on Minghella*, Preface by Sidney Pollack, Faber and Faber, London, 2005.
Monti P.,	*Ischia. Preistorica greca romana paleocristiana*.E.P.S. Napoli, 1968
Montanelli I.,	"Non immaginavo neanche di lontano che fosse il nostro ultimo incontro" in, *Angelo Rizzoli. 1889 1970*, RCS, Milano, 2000.
Morcellini M., Fatelli G.,	*Le scienze della comunicazione*, NIS, Roma, 1995.
Morgera D.,	*Il commenda- Angelo Rizzoli, l'uomo che*

"inventò" Un'isola La Città del sole, 2002, Napoli

Morin E., *Il cinema o l'uomo immaginario* Feltrinelli, Milano, 1982

Moscati M., *Il grande dizionario dei film* Hobby & Work Ed. Italiana, Bresso(MI), 1998

Mussolini V., in, *In cerca della formula di Vittorio Mussolini,* in, "Cinema", 1937 I 13-24, CSC.

Occhipinti P., "La sua più grande qualità era saper scegliere gli uomini", in, *AngeloRizzoli* 1889-1970, RCS, Milano, 2000.

Paliotti V., "Ischia e la canzone", in, Caprara V. (a cura di), *Ischia e il cinema* Il tirso, Ischia, 2002

Pecchinenda G., *Dell'identità*, Ipernmedium, Napoli, 1999.

Piselli F., *Parentela ed emigrazione*, Einaudi, Torino, 1981.

Poppi R., Pecorari M. *Dizionario del Cinema Italiano. I film dal 1960 al 1969*, Vol 3, Gremese, Roma, 2007.

Poppi R., Pecorari M. *Dizionario del Cinema Italiano.I film dal 1970 al 1979*, Vol 4 Tomo 1, Vol 4, Tomo 2, Gremese, 1996.

Pravadelli V., (a cura di) *Visconti a Volterra. La genesi di vaghe stelle dell'orsa*, Lindau, Torino, 2000.

Prisco M., "Il mio primo incontro con Angelo Rizzoli", in, Angelo Rizzoli, RCS, 2000, cit.

Pugliese E., *L'Italia tra migrazioni internazionali e migrazioni interne*, Il Mulino, Bologna, 2002.

Putnam R.D.,	*La tradizione civica nelle regioni italiane*, Mondadori, Milano, 1993.
Ragone G.,	*Psicosociologia dei consumi*, ISEDI, Milano, 1974.
Read P.P.,	"Alec Guinness. The Authorised Biography", Simon & Schuster, New York, 2003
Real Brian,	Conversazione privata, svoltasi nella Hall dell'Albergo Terme della Regina Isabella, in Lacco Ameno, nel luglio del 2006.
Ridgway D.,	*L'alba della Magna Grecia* 2° edizione, Biblioteca archeologica Longanesi & C, 1992
Royster F.T.,	*Becoming Cleopatra. The Shifting Image of an Icon*, Palgrave, Macmillan, New York, 2003.
Rossi Doria M.,	*Gli uomini e la storia*, Laterza, Bari, 1990.

Russo P.,	*Storia generale del cinema* Orsa Maggiore Editore, Milano, 1987
Saraceno P.,	*Il nuovo meridionalismo*, Quaderni del trentennale 1975 2005, Istituto Italiano Studi Filosofici, Napoli, 2005.
Sardella F.,	(a cura di) *Architettura d'Ischia* Analisi, Edizioni Castello Aragonese, Ischia, 1985
Saussure F. de,	Corso di linguistica generale, Laterza, Bari, 1967.
Serra P.,	*Bibliografia Isclana* Repertorio bibliografico generale Dell'isola d'Ischia. Ente Autonomo Valorizzazione isola d'Ischia, Napoli, 1966
Sikov E.,	*Mr. Strangelove. A Biography of Peter*

	Seller, Hyperion, New York, 2002
Spinazzola V.,	in, il mestire del critico, in, "*Cinema nuovo*", 1966, N° 179-184
Stampleton M.,	*Il grande libro della mitologia Greca e romana.*
Serven-Schreiber E.,	Arnaldo Mondadori editore, 1979
Tavernier B.,	"*Cinema*" '61 Parigi, 1961.
Toynbee A.J.	Civiltà al paragone, Bompiani, Milano, 2003.
Trigilia C.,	*Sviluppo senza autonomia. Effetti perversi delle politiche nel mezzogiorno*, Il Mulino, Bologna, 1994.
Truppi C.,	*La città del progetto*, Liguori, Napoli, 1999.
Truppi C.,	*Tra costruzione e progetto*, Angeli, Milano, 1991.

Visconti L., *Vaghe stelle dell'orsa*, Cappelli, Bologna, 1965.

Volpe A., *Il ciclo di vita delle località turistiche*, Angeli, Milano, 2004.

Vuoso U., *Di fuoco, di mare e di acque bollenti Leggende tradizionali dell'isola d'Ischia* Imagaenaria, Ischia, 2002

Walker A., *Vivien, The Life of Vivien Leigh* Weindenfeld & Nicolson, New York, 1987.

Wladimir F., *L'isola d'Ischia e le sue sorgenti* Barano, Casamicciola, Forio, Ischia, Lacco Ameno, Serrara Fontana. H.Bernard Frenkel Editrice Torre del Greco. Nuova guida 2 edizione 1929

CONSULTED WEBSITES

http://www.bdp.it/namm0010/buonop/flkem.htm
http://www.ischiafilm.it/films.html
http://premioischia.it/villa.phtml
http://premioischia.it/storia.phtml
http://www.larassegnadiischia.it/Libri/testi/edrassegna/paglacco60.htm
http://web.tiscali.it/capriottialessandro/rizzoli.htm
http://www.comunelaccoameno.it/museo_rizzoli/rizzoli_lacco.asp
http://www.rscmediagroup.it/corporate/profilo/profilostoricors.php
http://pointel.it/ischiamondo/sito_maggio/html/decima.html
http://pointel.it/ischiamondo/sito_giugno/html/nona.html
http://pointel.it/ischiamondo/sito_giugno/html/undicesima.html
http://www.dweb.repubblica.it/archivio_d/1999/0907/rubriche/libri/06216662.html
http://www.bdp.it/namm0009/pithek/attcost.html
http://www.bdp.it/namm0009/pithek/pithek.html
http://www.bdp.it/namm0009/pithek/origini.html
http://www.bdp.it/namm0009/pithek/micenei.html
http://www.bdp.it/namm0009/pithek/euboici.html
http://www.bdp.it/namm0009/pithek/linguapt.html
http://www.bdp.it/namm0009/pithek/scavi.html
http://www.bdp.it/namm0009/pithek/pntchiar.html
http://www.bdp.it/namm0009/pithek/mitilegg.html
http://digilander.libero.it/axell82/ilcastello2.htm
http://net.onion.it/ischia/html/ischia.html
http://chartitalia.blogspot.com/2005/09/classifica-film-stagione-195758.html
http://www.viaggi24.ilsole24ore.com/repository/articoli/2005/04/27/ischia_location_da_film.594304.php?ppid=811008

http://webreview.liberta.it/asp/default.asp?IDG=101720
http://it.wikipedia.org/wiki/Location
www.cineturismo.it
www.ischiafilmfestival.com
IschiaCity.it

FILMOGRAPHY

Here we present a repertoire of the main cinematographic works shot on the island of Ischia. Basic information about each film is listed: year of production, nationality, direction, protagonists. In several cases, we also summarize the essential elements of the plot. When the plot of the movie is not mentioned, it is because we discussed it more or less in the previous parts of the book.

Il Corsaro nero
by Amleto Palermi
pr. Giorgio Genesi per gli Artisti Associati (1936); *re.* Amleto Palermi; *sogg.* tratto dal romanzo omonimo di Emilio Salgari: Vaclar Vich, *mus* di Alessandro Cicognini *a.re.* Giorgio Bianchi, *int* Ciro Verrotti.

Il Dottor Antonio
by Enrico Guazzoni
pr, Pietro Mander per la Mander-film (1937); *re.* Enrico Guazroni; *sogg.* tratto dal romanzo omonimo di Giovanni Ruffini nella riduzione di Gherardo Gherardi; *scen.* G. Ghe-rardi, E. Guazzoni, Gino Talamo; *dir. fot.* Massimo Terzano; *tnus.* Umberto Mancini, Giovanni Fusco; *mo.* G, Talamo; *scg.* e *co.* E. Guazzoni; *d. pr.* Gustavo Serena; *a. re.* G. Talamo; *op,* Goffredo Bellisa-rio; *fo.* Giacomo Pitzorno; *ini.* Ennio Cerlesì (*// dottor Antonio),* Maria Gambarelli *(missLucy),* Lamberto Picasso *(sir John Davenne),* Mino Doro *(Prospero),* Tina Zucchi *(Speranza),* Vinicio Sofia *(Turi),* Margherita Bagni *(miss Elizabetti),* Claudio Ermelli *(Tom),* Luigi Pavese *(Aubrey),* Giannìnà Chiantoni *(Rosa),* Romolo Costa *(Hasling),* Augusto Di Giovanni *(Ferdinando 11° dì Napoli),* Guido Celano *(Domenico Morelli),* Enzo Biliotti *(Carlo Poerio),*

Alfredo Menichelli *(Luigi Settembrini),* Massimo Pianforini *(Lord Cleverton),* Rocco D'Assunta *(Michele Pìrontf),* Vittorio Bianchi *(il doti. Stage),* Alfredo Robert *(// generale Nunziante),* Enzo De Felice *(Romeo),* Olinto Cristina *(l'ambasciatore inglese a Napoli),* Giuseppe Duse *(ufficiale borbonico),* Achille Majeronì *(l'avvocato dell'accusa),* Giovanni Onorato *(un oratore in piazza),* Aristide Garbini, Pietro Tordi *(due cospiratori),* Omelia Da Vasto, Giovanni Ferrari, Luigi Esposito, Ermena Malusardi, Cesare Fantoni, Michele Malaspina, Gilberto Macellari, Alessio Gobbi, Giovanni Ferraguti, Alessandra Varna. Nota: Distr. Manderfilm.

Duration: 98 minutes. The movie was filmed in Pisorno cinema establishments in Tirrenia. (Cf., Chiti Lancia, 1993, cit.,)

Vampiro dell'isola (Isle of the Deal)
USA 1945 re. Mark Robson. Scen. Ardel Wray e Josef Mischel. Con Boris Karloff, Ellen Drew, Mar Cramer, Katherine Emery, Alan Napier, Jason Robards sr.

L'acqua li portò via
by Rate Furlan;
Re sogg. scen.Rate Furlan; Dir.fot. Carlo Ciarlino; Musiche R. Furlan; a.re. Guido Pacifico;
d.pr.Mario Pellegrino; int. Tecla Scarano e attori non protagonisti. Filmed in 1949 and never shown to the public "because the producers went to court to resolve their disputes based on financial shares and related gains"—a declaration made by R. Furlan. No one has ever seen the movie.

Il Mulatto
by Francesco De Robertis
pr. Scalerà Film, (1950); *re.* Francesco De Robertis; *sogg. e scen.* F. De Robertis; *dir.fot.* Carlo Sellerò; *mus.* Annibale Bizzelli; *mo.* Loris Bellero; *scg.* naturale; *coli. re.* Leonardo De Mitri; *d.pr.* Franco Magli; *ass.re.* Luciano Volpati; *i.p.* Nino Milano; *ass.op.* Dino Reni;/o. Tulio Parmeggiani; *c.s.e.* R. Buccali; *int.* Umberto Spadaro *(don Gennaro),* Renato Baldini *(Matteo Belfiore),* Iole Fierro *(Catari),* Mohamed H. Hussein *(lo zio di Angelo),* Giulia Melidoni, R. De Angelis, il piccolo Angelo Maggio *(Angelo).*

Campane a martello
by Luigi Zampa
pr. Carlo Ponti per Lux Film, (1948); *re.* Luigi Zampa; *sogg. e scen.* Piero Tellini; *dir.fot.* Carlo Montuori; *mus.* Nino Rota dir. da Franco Ferrara; *mo.* Eraldo Da Roma; *scg.* Piero Gherardi; *d.pr.* Bruno Todini; *a.re.* Mauro Bolognini, Giuseppe Colizzi; *i.p.* Nicolo Po-milia, Pasquale Misiano; *s.ed.* Paolo Heusch; *op.* Mario Montuori, Giorgio Orsini». Ennio Sensi, Mario Amari; *tr.* Alberto De Rossi; *int.* Gina Lollobrigida *(Agostina),* Yvonne Sanson *(Australia),* Carlo Romano *(il maresciallo),* Carlo Giustini *(Marco),* Clelia Matania *(Bianca),* Ernesto Almirante *(i lpossidente),* Agostino Salvietti, Gino Saltamerenda, Salvatore Arcidiacono *(il farmacista),* Ada Colangeli, Pasquale Misiano, Vittoria Febbi, Francesco Santoro, Vincenzo Mazzola, Carlo Pisacane, con Eduardo De Filippo *(don Andrea).* Nota: Distr. Lux Film. Reg. Cin.co 751. Incasso: 113.750.000.

La Scogliera del peccato
by Roberto Bianchi Monterò
pr. International Urania Film (Napoli), 1950; *re.* Roberto Monterò; *sogg.* Enzo Avitabile; *scen.* Fulvio Palmieri, Mario Galatrona, E. Avitabile, R. Monterò; *dir.fot.* Carlo Nebiolo; *mus.* Alberto De Castello dir. da Ugo Giacomozzi; •*mo.* Guido Bertoli; *ass.mo.* Pietro Armarmi; *scg.* Alfredo Mentori; *d.pr.* Mario Pellegrino; *a.re.* Gennaro Balistrte" ri; *ass.re.* Enzo Avitabile; *s.p.* Amedeo Puthod; *s.ed.* Enza Campanaio; *op.* Giuseppe Aquari; *ass.op.* Luigi Di Giorgio; *tr.* Antonio Marini; *ini.* Gino Cervi *(Silvano)*, Margaret Genske *(Stella)*, Delia Scala *(Anna)*, Otello Toso *(Michele)*, Ermanno Randi *(Paolo)*, Leopoldo Valentini *(Giovanni-nò)*, Giga Solbelli *(Maria)*, Amedeo Novelli [Trilli], Gustavo Serena, il piccolo Augusto Ciabatti *(Schizzetto)*, Virginia Balistrieri, Siva Fazi. Nota: Distr. Regionale. Reg. Gin.co 891. Durata 93'. Incasso: 105.000.000.

Il corsaro dell'isola verde
by Robert Siodmak,
original title "The crimson Pirate", *dur* 104, *orig* Gran Bretagna USA, *gen* avventura *form* Technicolor, *pr* Harold hecht/norma pictures, *re* Robert Siodmak, *sogg* Roland kibbee, *scen.* Roland kibbee, Burt Lancaster Waldo Salt, *dir fot* Otto Heller, *mus.* William Alwyn, *mo* Jack Harris, *scen* Paul Sheriff, attori: Eva Bartok: Consuelo; Leslie Bradley: Barone Don J. Gruda; Nick Cravat: Ojo; Margot Grahame: Bianca; James Hayter: Prof Eli Prudence burt Lancaster: Capitano Vallo; Christopher Lee: addetto; Frederick Leicester: El Libre; Eliot Makeham: governatore; Frank Pettingill: Colonnello; Noel Purcell: Pablo Murphy; Torin Thatcher: Humble Bellows; Dana Wynter: Senorita.

Città canora
(Italia, 1952, b/n, 56') di Mario Costa.
Con Maria Fiore, Giacomo Rondinella, Nadia Gray, Tina Pica, Giovanni Grasso, mirko Ellis, Giuseppe Porelli, Dante Maggio, Beniamino Maggio, Carlo Romano, Paolo Borboni, Lella Calabrese.

Mostro dell'isola
by Roberto Bianchi Monterò
pr. Fortunato Misiano per Romana Film, (1953); *re.* Roberto Bianchi Monterò; *sogg.* Carlo Lombardi; *scen.* Alberto Vecchietti; *dir.fot.* Augusto Tiezzi; *mus.* Carlo innocenzi (canzoni di Innoccnzi-Rivi cantate da Franca Marzi e Giacomo Rondinel'la); *mo.* Jolanda Benvenuti; *scg.* Alfredo Mentori; *urr.* Armando Su-scipi; *d.pr.* Franco Misiano; *a.re.* Giulio Perrone; *i.p.* Alberto Cinquini; *s.p.* Pasquale Misiano; *cons.milit.* cap. Salvatore Scibetta; *op.* Angelo Lotti; *ass. op.* Nino Malchiodi; *s.ed.* Maria Grazia Bodro; *fo.* Oscar Di Santo; *tr.* Luigi Sfuriale; *ini.* Boris Karloff *(don Gaetano),* Franca Marzi *(Gloria D'Auro),* Renato Vicario *(ten. Mario Andreani),* Iole Fierro *(Giulia),* Patrizia Remiddi *(la piccola Fiorella),* Carlo Buse *(Poster),* Giuseppe Chinnici *(maresciallo Antonio Coreani),* Giulio Battiferri *(il rapitore della bambina),* Domenico (Mimmo) De Ninno *(l'uomo di Fazzuoli),* Alberto D'Amario *(Morozzi),* Germana Paolieri *(Adalgisa),* Giuseppe Addobbati *(direttore dancing "Sirena"),* Giara Gamberini *(la contessa),* Salvatore Scibetta *(colonello della finanza),* Angelo Dessy *(un contrabbandiere),*
Gianni Breschi, Kitty Vinciguerra, Bruna Camerini, il lupo Zar. Nota: Distr. Romana Film. Reg. Cin.co 1.346. Incasso: 87.500.000. Studi: Cinecittà. Reg.

sonore R.C.A. Pellicola: Ferrania Panerò *CI.* Durata 90'.

Lacrime d'amore
by Pino Mercanti
pr. Fortunato Misiano -per Romana Film, (1954); *re.* Pino Mercanti; *sogg.* Michele Galdieri dalla canzone «Ddoje lacreme»; *scen.* M. Galdieri, Franco Perroni; *dir.fot.* Augusto Tiezzi; *mus.* Carlo Innocenzi; *mo.* Jolanda Benvenuti; *scg.* Sergio Baldacchini; *co.* Maria Rosaria Grimi; *arr.* Camillo Del Signore; *o.g.* Umberto Scarpelli; *d.pr.* Franco Misiano; *a.re.* Giuseppe Mariani; *i.p.* Pasquale Misiano; *op.* Marcelle Gatti; *fo.* Pietro Ortolani; *Int.* Achille Togliani *(Mario Benetti),* Ratina Ranieri *(Grazia Montalto),* Bianca Fusari *(Rosetta),* Otello Toso *(Davide Maltolto),* Enrico Glori *(comm. Goebritz),* Umberto Spadaro, Rita Rosa, Incida Meroni, Dina De San-tis, Nadia Bianchi, Mimo Billi, Roberto Paoletti, John Kitzmiller, Carlo Romano, Nada Cortese, Piero Giagnoni. Nota: Distr. Sicien Film. Durata 90'. Rcg, Ck.co 1.510. Studi: Incir-De Paolis. Incasso: 143.169.000.

Suor Letizia
by Mario Camerini
pr, Sandro Pallavicini per Rizzoli Film, Pallavicini, (1956); *re.* Mario Camerini;
sogg. Cesare Zavattini, M. Camerini da un'idea di Antonio Altoviti e Giosué Ri-manelli; *scen.* Leo Benvenuti, Piero De Bernardi, M. Camerini, Siro Angeli, En-nio De Concini, Ugo Guerra, Mario Guerra, Aldo Paladini, Vito Blasi, Am-leto Micozzi, Virgilio Tosi; *dir.fot.* Gian-ni Di Venanzo; *mus.* Angelo Francesco Lavagnino; *mo.* Giuliana Attenni; *scg.* Franco Lolli; *co.* e *arr.* Piero Tosi; *d.pr.* Franco Magli, Emo Bistolfi; *a.re.* Otto Pellegrini; *s.p.* Oscar

Brazzi; *s.ed.* Carla Fierro; *op. Erica* Menczer; *ass.op.* Dario Di Palma; *fo.* Attilio Nicolai; *tr.* Alberto De Rossi;
int. Anna Magnani *(suor Letizia),* Eleo-nora Rossi Drago *(Assunta),* Antonio Ci-fariello *(Pappino),* Piero Boccia *(ilpiccolo Salvatore, figlio di Assunta),* Bianca Doria *(Concetta),* Luisa Rossi *(una suora),* Lina Tartara Minora *(suora anziana),* Bruna Cealti, Margò Mannelly, Sara Simoni, Ugo Mari, Aldo Pini, Aristide Catoni, Paolo Ferrara, Nicola Maldacea jr., Leonilde Montesi *(altra suora anziana),* Roberto Rai, Cristina Cataldi, Nan-da Primavera, Emma Baron, Eugenio Galadini, Bruna Carletti, Miriam Pisani, Attilio Torelli, Salvo Libassi, Giancarlo Zarfati, Marisa Belli, Giuseppe Picchi. Nota: Distr. Ceiad. Anna Magnani ottenne, con questo film, il suo quinto Nastro d'argento. L'anno precedente aveva vinto l'Oscar *(La rosa tatuata).* Sottotitolo // *più grande amore.* Durata 98'. Reg. Cin-.co 1.814. Incasso: 356.000.000.

Scampolo - Sissi a Ischia
by Giorgio Bianchi
pr. Lorenzo Pegoraro per Peg Produzione Film (Roma), Gite Film (Parigi), 1953; *re.* Giorgio Bianchi; *sogg.* dalla commedia di Dario Niccodemi; *scen.* Aldo De Benedetti, Oreste Biancoli, Giorgio Prosperi, G. Bianchi; *dir.fot.* Mario Albertelli; *mus.* Nino Rota dir. da Franco Ferrara; *mo.* Gabriele Varriale; *scg.* Mario Chiari; *a.scg.* Marcelle Torri; *arr.* Mario Garbuglia; *o.g.* Lorenzo Pegoraro; *d.pr.* Luigi Giacosi; *a.re.* Fede Arnaud;/o. Bruno Brunacci, Alberto Bartolomei; *int.* Maria Fiore *(Scampolo),* Henri Vi-dal *(ing. Tifo Scacchi),* Cosetta Greco *(signora Bernini),* Paolo Stoppa *(signor Bernini),* Georgette Anys *(la stiratrice),* Ariette Poirier *(Franca),* Paolo Panelli *(Orazio),* Brunella

Bovo *(Augusta)*, Umberto Spadaro *(commissario)*, Giuseppe Porcili, Nando Bruno, Galeazze Benti, Ada Colangeli, Nerone Locateli!, la barboncina Jolly.
Nota: Distr. Enic. Durata 90'. Reg. Gin.co 1.282. In Ferraniacolor. Incasso: 152.000.000.

Vacanze a Ischia
by Mario Camerini
pr. Rizzoli Film (Roma), Francinex (Parigi), Bavaria Film (Monaco), 1957; *re.* Mario Camerini; *sogg.* Leo Benvenuti, Piero De Bernardi; *scen.* L. Benvenuti, P. De Bernardi, M. Camerini, Pasquale Festa Campanile, Massimo Franciosa; *dir.fot.* Otello Colangeli; *mus.* Alessandro Cicognini; *mo.* Giuliana Attenni; *scg.* Castone Carsetti; *co.* Piero Tosi; *arr.* Giorgio Pes; *d.pr.* Franco Magli; *a.re.* Paolo Heusch, Otto Pellegrini; *s.p.* Mario Abussi; *op.* Arturo Zavattini; *fo.* Carlo Palmieri; *tr.* Alberto De Rossi; *int.* Vittorio De Sica *(ing. Occhipinti)*, Isabelle Corey *(Caterina Lissotto)*, Antonio Cifariello *(Antonio)*, Nadia Gray *(Carla Occhipinti)*, Myriam Bru *(Denise Tissot)*, Paolo Stoppa *(avv. Appicciato)*, Susanne Cramer *(Antonietta, infermiera)*, Raf Mattioli *(Salvatore, la guida)*, Peppino De Filippo *(Battistella)*, Mamizio Arena *(Franco)*, Bernard Dhéran *(Pierre Tissot)*, Nino Besozzi *(Guido Lucarelli)*, Huberl Von Mcye-rinck *(col. Manfredi)*, Laura Carli *(signora Lucarelli)*, Giuseppe Porcili *(il giudice)*, Giampiero Littera *(Benito)*, Guglielmo Inglese *(un magistrato)*, Enio Girolami *(Furio)*, Eduardo Passarelli, Michele Riccardini, Angela Maria Lavagna, Arturo Criscuolo, Bruna Cealti.
Nota: Distr. Cineriz. Reg. Cin.co 1.925. In Totalscope-Eastmancolor. Incasso: 736.413.000. Titolo francese *Vacances a Ischia*. Titolo tedesco *Ferien auf der Sonneninsel*.

Delitto in pieno sole (Plein soleil)
In pieno sole, Francia 1959, col, 120. *re.* Renè Clement. *Int.* Alain Delon, Marie Laforet, Maurice Ronet, Elvire Popesco, Erno Crisa, Ave Ninchi (Chiti E., Poppi R., 1991, cit.).

Appuntamento a Ischia
by Mario Mattoli
pr. Romano Dandi per Serena Film, (1960); *re.* Mario Mattoli; *sogg. e scen.* Vittorio Metz, Roberto Gianviti; *dir. fot.* Roberto Gerardi, Marco Scarpelli; *mus.* Gianni Ferrio, (le canzoni cantate da Domenico Modugno sono incise su dischi Fonit, ed. mus. Accordo, Milano; Mina canta «La nonna Magdalena» di Misa, Pallavicini, «Il ciclo in una stanza», di Mogol, Toang [Gino Paoli], «Una zebra a pois» di Luttazzi, incise su dischi Italdischi); *mo.* Adriana Novelli; *scg.* Flavio Mogherini; *co.* Vera Marzot; *d. pr.* Romano Dandi; *a. re.* Gabriele Palmieri; */. p.* Antonio Girasante; *s. ed.* Mìrella Gamacchio; *op.* Idelmo Simonelli, Ennio Guarnieri; o. Giovanni Rossi; *tr.* Efrade Titì',*parr.* Maria Miccinelli; *se.* Cristiano Civirani;
ini. Domenico Modugno *(Domenico, detto Mimmo),* Antonella Lualdi *(Mirella),* Maria Letizia Gazzoni *(Letìzia),* Linda Christian *(Mercedes),* Carlo Croccolo *(Cadetto),* Yvette Masson *(Veronique),* Pietro De Vico *(il pianista),* Elsa Vazzoler *(Anna),* Ugo D'Alessio *(Antonio),* Alberto Talegalli *(direttore zoo),* Mario Castellani *(l'agente musicale),* Carlo Tarante *(Gennarino),* Mimo Siili *(maresciallo della finanza)* , Toni Ucci *(uomo seduto al tavolo di un bar),* Ughetto Bertucci *(il tassista),* ElviraTonelli *(la fioraia),* Paolo Ferrari *(Paolo),* Alberto Sorrentino *(il portiere di via Margutta),* con Franco Franchi e Ciccio Ingrassia *(i due contrabbandieri*

siciliani), Pippo Franco *(un chitarrista)* e con la partecipazione di Mina *(se stessa).*
Nota: Distr. Cineriz. Durata: 91'. Reg. Cin.co 2.332. In Eastmancolor - Total-scope. Colore della Tecnostampa. Scudi: Titanus. Titolo in Francia *Rendez-vous a Ischia.* Incasso: 209.000.000.

Morgan il pirata
by Primo Zeglio
pr. Lux Film, Adelphia Cin.ca (Roma), C.ie Cin.que de France (Parigi), 1960; *re.* Primo Zeglio; *sup. re.* Andre De Toth; *sogg. e scen.* Filippo Sanjust, P. Zeglio, Attilio Riccio, A. De Toth; *dir. fot.* Tonino Delli Colli; *mus.* Franco Mannino; mo. Maurizio Lucidi; *scg.* Gianni Polidori; *co.* Filippo Sanjust; *a. co.* Franca Mandelli; *o. g.* Nicolo Porni-lia; *d. pr.* Aldo Pomilia; *a. re.* Alberto Cardor.e; *i. p.* Roberto Onori, Luciano Della Pria; *s. p.* Giuseppe Rispoli; *op.* Mario Pastorini; *ass. op.* Gino Santini, Giovacchino Sofia; *m. armi* Enzo Mu-sumeci Greco; *eff. sp.* Eros Baciucchi; *fo.* Fausto Ancillai; *tr.* Anacleto Giusti-ni; *parr.* Lina Cassini; *ini.* Steve Reeves *(Henry Morgan),* Va-lerie Lagrange *(Ynez),* Cheto Alonso *(Conception),* Ivo Garrani *(il governatore),* Armand Mestral *(Pietro Nau, detto Olonese),* Giulio Bosetti *fiordMo-dyford),* Lydìa Alfonsi *(Maria),* Giorgio Ardisson *(Walter),* Angelo Zanolli *(David),* Dino Malacrida *(LeDue),* Ani-ta Tedesco.
Nota: Distr. Lux Film. Durata: 103'. Reg. Cin.co 2.284. Sincr. Titanus. Reg. sonora Fonolux. Titolo francese *Capitarne Morgan.* TitoloU. S. A. (distr. Joseph E. Levine/ M.G.M., 1961) *Morgan thePirate.* Incasso: 618.000.000.

Cleopatra
Usa 1963, col 243, re. Joseph L. Mankiewicz. Int Elisabeth Taylor, Richard Burton, Rex Harrison, Pamela Brown, Gorge Cole, Hume Cronyn, Cesare Danova, Martin Landau, Roddy Mc Dowall.

Diciottenni al sole
by Camillo Mastrocinque
pr. Isidoro Broggi e Renato Libassi per D.D.L. Cin.ca, (1962); *re.* Camillo Mastrocinque; *sogg. e scen.* (Franco) Castellano e Pipolo [Giuseppe Moccia]; *dir. fot.* Riccardo Pallottini; *mus.* Ennio Morricone (ed. mus.R. C. A.), coni 4 + 4 di Nora Oriandi; *mo.* Gisa Radicchi Levi; *scg. e arr.* Aurelio Crugnola; *co.* Giuliano Papi; *d. pr.* Gianni Minervinì; *a. re.* Nino Zanchin; *l'. p.* Nino Fruscella; *s. p.* Nico Benetti; *s. ed.* Carla Fieno; *op.* Castone Di Giovannij/o. Alessandro Sarandrea; *tr.* Sergio Angeloni; *parr.* Maria MiccinelH; *inf.* Catherine Spaak *(Nicole)*, Gianni Garko *(Nicola)*, Spiros Focas *(Nonni)*, Luisa Mattici! *(Vania)*, Fabrizio Capucci *(Massimo)*, Giampiero Littera *(Carlo)*, Stelvio Rosi *(Giorgio Mazzoli)*, Eleonora Morana *(turista)*, Mario Bre-ga *(Gennarino)*, Ignazio Leone *(animatore dell'albergo)*, Lars Bloch *(Lars)*, Oliviero Prunas *(Bruno)*, Margrete Robsahm *(Evelyn)*, Paolo De Bellis, Paola Del Bosco, Loris Bazzocchi, Annamaria Ubaldi, Bruna Mori, con Franco Giacobini *(commissario)*, Gabriele Antonini *(Letto)* e Lisa Castoni *(Franca)*.
Nota: Distr. Astoria. Durata: 92', Reg. Gin.co 2.733. In Eastmancolor (schermo panoramico). Negativi e positivi: Staco Film. Sincr. Fono Roma. Dopp. C. D..C. Interni: Studi De Paolis, esterni ad Ischia. Incasso: 507.000.000. Canzoni inserite nel film: «Nicole» di Pilantra e Morricone, cantata da Gianni Meccia e Jìmmy Fontana; «Donna da morire», stessi

autori, cantata da Tony Del Monaco; «Go-kart», stessi autori, cantata da Gianni Morandi; «Twist n. 9» di Fontana e Morricone, cantata da Jimmy Fontana e Gianni Meccia; «Pinne, fucili ed occhiale» e «Guarda come dondolo» di Rossi, Vianello e Leonardi, cantate da Edoardo Vianello.

Caccia alla volpe
by Vittorio De Sica
pr, John Bryan per Compagnia Cin.ca Monterò (Roma), Nancy Enterprises (Londra), 1966; *re.* Vittorio De Sica; *sogg.* da una commedia di Neìl Simon; *scen.* Neil Simon; *coli. scen.* Cesare Zavattini; *dir. fot.* Leonida Barboni; *mus.* Piero Piccioni dir. da Ralph Ferrare (mus. ediz. U. S. A. di Burt Bacharach); *mo.* Adriana Novelli (ediz. U.S.A. Russell Lloyd); *scg.* Mario Garbuglia; *co.* Piero Tosi; *o. g.* Maurizio Lodi-Fé; *d. pr.* Grazio Tassara; *re. 2a unità* Richard Talmadge, Giorgio Stegani; *a. re.* Luisa Alessandri, Franco Girino; *i. p.* Angelo Binarelli; *s. p.* Valerio De Paolis; *s. ed.* Elvira D'Amico; *op.* Arturo Zavattini, Claudio Ragona;/*o.* Roberto Cuomo; *tr.* Amato Garbini, Stuart Freeborn; *eff. sp.* Joseph Nathanson; *Ut. testa* Maurice Binder (con un brano musicale di Hai David e B, Bacharach, cantato da P. Sellers e The Hofflcs); *int.* Peter Sellers *(Aldo Vannucd),* Victor Mature *(Tony Powell),* Britt Ekland *(Gina),* Akim Tamiroff *(Okra),* Paolo Stoppa *(Pollo),* Tino Buazzelii *(Siepi),* Maria Grazia Buccella *(la sorella di Okra),* Lidia Brazzi *(Teresa Vannucd),* Martin Balsam *(Harry),* Lando Buzzanca *(capitano di polizia Rizzato),* Vittorio De Sica *(lui stesso),* Mac Ronay *(Carlo),* Tiberio Murgia *(I° poliziotto),* Pier Luigi Pizzi *(il dottore),* Maurice Denham *(capo dell'Interpol),* Enzo Fiermonte *(Raymond),* Carlo Croccolo *(Salvatore),* Francesco De Leone *(2°. poliziotto),* Nino Musco *(il maggiore),*

Lino Matterà *(il cantante)*, Daniele Var-gas *(avvocato dell'accusa)*, Franco Sportelli *(un giudice)*, Carlo Pisacane *(altro giudice)*, Giustino Durano *(il critico)*, Mimmo Poli *(l'attore)*, Angelo Spaggiari *(Felix Kessler)*, Timothy Bateson *(Michael O'Reilly)*, David Lodge *(altro poliziotto)*, Roberto De Simone *(Marcel Vignon)*, Piero Gerliru, Daniela Igliozzi, Carlo Delle Piane, Nino Vin-gelli *(un altro giudice)*, Enrico Luzi *(il regista a via Veneto)*, Marcella Rovena *(moglie di Salvatore)*. Nota: Distr. Dear-U.A. Durata: lOO'. In Panavision-De Luxe Color (stampa Technicolor), Reg. Cin.co 3.557. Titolo inglese *After thè Fox*. Titolo francese *Le renard s'evade a 3 heures (o Un fa-meux renard)*. Incasso: 379.000.000.

Ischia operazione amore
by Vittorio Sala
pr. Luigi Rovere per Cineluxor, Rizzoli Film, (1966); *re.* Vittorio Sala; *sogg.* Luigi De Santis, Osvaldo De Micheli; *scen.* Adriano Baracco, Ugo Guerra, O. De Micheli, L. De Santis; *dir. fot.* Aldo Giordani; *mus.* Roberto Nicolosi dir. Autore (ed. mus. C. A. M.), la canzone «Nessun'altra che te» è composta e cantata da Tony Renis; *mo.* Tatiana Mori-gi; *ass. mo.* Nadia Mazzoni; *scg.* Otta-vio Scotti; *co.* Renato Beer; *ass.,co.* An-giolìna Menicbelli; *arr.* Oreste Sabatini; *se. tee.* Carlo Agate, Angelo Zambon; *d. pr.* Renato Panetuzzi; *a. re.* Gian Paolo Taddeini; *s. ed.* Maria Grazia Baldanello; *s. p.* Alberto Rovere; *amm..* Fernanda Ventimiglia; *s. amm.* Miriam Marchetti; *op.* Sergio Bergamini; *ass. op.* Franco Frazzi; Pietro Vesperini; *mie.* Giorgio Minoprio; *tr.* Duilio Giu-stini ; *porr.* Marcelle Di Paolo; *sarta* Va-leria Ferretti; *mix.* Mario Morigi;. *se.* Angelo Pennoni; *int.* Walter Chiari *(Enrico Tremalaterra)*, Graziella Granata *(Marina)*, Ingrid

Schòeller *(Ingrid)*, Oidi Perego *(Flavia Peruzzi)*, Hélène Chanci *(Beatrice)*, Evi Marandi *(Nennetla)*, Vittorio Caprioli *(barone Lo Russo)*, Tony Renis *(Marco)*, Angelo Infanti *(Peppiniello)*, Alberto Cevenini *(Luigi)*, Cadetto Sposilo *(maresciallo Francesco Capece)*, Ignazio Leone *(il prete)*, Anna Campori *(moglie di Gennaro)*, Rie [Riccardo Miniggio] *(Primo)*, Gian [Gian Fabio Bosco] *(Secondo)*, Adriana Pacchetti *(la turista americana)*, Umberto D'Orsi, Carletto Sposito, Ermelinda De Felice, Edda Ferronao, con Peppino De Filippo *(Gennaro Capotesta)*.

Nota: Distr. Cineriz. Reg. Gin.co 3.609. In Techniscope - Technicolor. Film d'esordio per i comici Rie e Gian. Incasso: 343.000.000 (Cf., Poppi R., Pecorari M., 2007, cit.).

"Che cosa è successo tra tuo padre e mia madre?" O "Avanti"
by Billy Wilder
pr. Alberto Grimaldi per P.E.A. (Roma), Miriseli Corporation. (U.S.A.), 1972; *re.* Billy Wilder; y *sogg.* dalla commedia «Avanti!» di Samuel Taylor prodotta a New York da Morris Jacobs e Jerome Whyte in coli, con Richard Rodgers; *scen.* B. Wilder, I.A.L. Diamond, Luciano Vincenzoni; *dir. fot.* Luigi Kuveiller (Mario Damicelli per foto aeree); *mus.* Carlo Rustichelli dir. da Giancarlo Plenizio; canzoni; «'A tazza;» caffè» di G. Capaldo e V. Passone; «La luna» di D. Backy, Detto Mariano; «Palcoscenico» di E. Bonagura, A. Giannini, S. Bruni; «Senza fine» di G. Paoli; «Gore 'ngrato» di Cordi-ferro e Cardillo; «Un'ora sola ti vorrei» di Marchetti; *mo.* Ralph E. Winthers; *ass. mo.* Claudio Cutry. Bobbie Shapiro; *scg.* Ferdinando; Scarfiotti; *ass. scg.* Osvaldo Desideri; *arr.* Nedo Azzini; *co.* Annalisa; Nasalli Rocca; *ass. co.* Paola Comencini;

d. pr. Alessandro Von Norman; *a. re.* Rinaldo Ricci; *s. ed.* yvonne Axworthy; */. p.* Ennio Onorati, Peter Sheperd; *casting* Isa Bartalini; *tr.* Franco Preda (Harry Rey per J. Lemmon); *parr.* Adalgisa Favella; *mo. mus.* Serge Brand; *mo. suono* Frank Warner; *fa.* Basii Fen-ton Smith; *e. s. m.* Sergio Emidi; *e.* Sergio Coletta; */. se.* Paul Ronald; *dir. dial.* Raffaele Mottura; *uff. st.* Chuck Painter, Nella Garoz-zo; *int.* Jack Lemmon *(Wendell Armoni-star)*, Juliet Mills *(Pamela Figgati)*, Clive Revill *(Carlo Carlucci)*, Edward Andrews *(Joseph C. Blodoeti)*, Pippo Franco *(Matarazzo, custode obitorio)*, Lino Coletta *(Cipriani, il suo assistente)*, Franco Acampora *(Armando Trotta)*, Franco Angrisano *(Arnaldo Trotta)*, Giselda Castrini *(Anna, cameriera)*, Gianfranco Barra *(Bruno, cameriere)*, Sergio Bruni *(cantante)*, Maria Rosa Sclauzero *(hostess)*, Raffaele Motto-la *(agente)*, Antonino Faà Di Bruno *(congierge hotel)*, Giacomo Rizzo *(barman)*, Melù Valente *(hostess)*, Aldo Rendine *(Rossi, funzionario eliporto)*, Guidarino Guidi *(inoltre hotel)*, Franca Sciutto, Gianni Pulo-ne, Vanti Somer, Janet Agren, Giuseppe Giudio.
Nota: Distr. United Artists. Durata 146'. In De Lu'xe Color, stampa Technicolor. Reg. Gin.co 5.223. Titolo americano e internazionale *Avanti!* Incasso: 410.000.000.

La svergognata
Produzione Italia 1974, re. Giuliano Biagetti. Interpreti: Barbara Bouchet, Stefano Amato, Leonora Fani, Philippe Leroy, durata 90
Trama: Nino, an industrialist from Milan, arrives on the island of Ischia for a vacation together with his wife, Clara, and his daughter, Ornella. Several people are staying in the same hotel, among which Fabio stands out, a writer who is suffering a bout of

depression. Fabio was the lover of Mrs. Bernardi five years earlier and is now the faithful companion of the actress Silvia. Ornella, encouraged by her friend Giusi, soon gets tired of meeting up with the boys who are in their company. Commento critico: Esordio, poco brillante, a dire la verità, di Eleonora Cristofani in arte Leonora Fani (Cf., Poppi R., Pecorari M., 1996, cit.)

Arrivano Joe e Margherito
Italia, 1974, col 105)
by Giuseppe Coalizzi.
Con Keith Carradine, Tom Skerrit, Sybil Danning, Pepe Calvo.(Cf., Mereghetti, 2002, cit.)

La professoressa di scienze naturali.
Italia 1976, col 90', Michele Massimo Tarantini. Con Lilli Carati, Michele Gammino, Marco Gelardini, Alvaro Vitali, Mario Carotenuto, Ria De Simone, Gianfranco D'Angelo, Giacomo Rizzo, Gianfraco Barra, Gastone Pesucci. (Cf., Mereghetti, 2002, cit).

La vergine il toro e il capricorno
by Luciano Martino
pr. Luciano Martino per Devon Cin.ca, Medusa Distribuzione, 1976; *re.* Luciano Martino; *sogg.* L. Martino, Francesco Milizia; *scen.* Cesare Frugoni, L. Martino, F. Milizia; *dir. fot.* Gioncarlo Ferrando; *mus.* Franco Pisano; *mo.* Eugenio Alabiso; *ass. mo.* Teresa Negozio; *a. ass. ino.* Marco Roselli; *scg.* Francesco Calabrese; *ass. scg.* Franco Marino; *co.* Luciana Marinucci; *ass. co.* Evy Farinelli; *o. g.* Gianni Saragò; *a. re.* Franco Girino; *s. ed.* Mirella Roy Malatesta; *op.* Claudio Morabito; *ass. op.* Rolando Ferrano; *fo.* Raffaele De Luca; *mie.* Angelo Amatulli; *mix.* Bruno Moreal; *tr.* Franco Schioppa; *parr.* Marcelle Longhi; *se.* Francesco Narducci; *se. tee.*

Franco Pirri; *amm.* Maria Spera; *cass.* Antonio Saragò; *int.* Edwige Fenech *(Gioia Ferretti),* Alberto Lionello *(danni, suo marito).* Aldo Maccione *(barone Felice Spezzaferri),* Olga Bisera *(Enrico),* Ray Lovelock *(Patrizio Marchi),* Lia Tanzi *(Ltiisa),* Alvaro Vitali *(Alvaro, cameriere e fattorino),* Erna Schurer *(turista tedesca con Patrizio),* Michele Cammino *(Raffaele, detto Fefé),* Mario Carotenuto *(commendatore Pietro Guzzoni),* Giacomo Rizzo *(Peppino Ruotalo),* Fiammetta Baralla *(Aìda, la domestica),* Gianfranco Barra *(Alberto Scapicolli),* Lars Bloch *(professore americano),* Sabina De Guida *(marchesa al ballo),* Ria De Simone *(signora Scapicolli),* Adriana Pacchetti *(moglie di Guzzoni),* Riccardo Cartone *(marito di Enrico),* Cesarina Gheraldi *(Zoraide, madre di Gianni),* Gabriella Lepori *(segretaria di Gianni),* Patrizia Webley [Patrizia De Rossi] *(moglie di Raffaele),* Ugo Bologna *(commendatore Ferretti, padre di Gianni),* Tiberio Murgia *(il maresciallo),* Sophia Lombardo *(altra segretaria di danni).* Dante Cleri *(il gelataio).* Laura Trotter *(Helen, segretaria del professore),* Anna Melita, Pinuccìo Ardia, Tony Morgan, Beniamino Sterpetti. Nota: Distr. Medusa. Durata 90'. In Eastmancolor, colore L. V. (Luciano Vittori). Esterni a Roma e Ischia. Reg. Cìn.co 6.267. (Cf., Poppi R., Pecorari M., 1996, cit.)

Rolf
Italia 1983
Regia Mario Siciliano
Cast: Tony Marsina, Ketty Nicholas, Tony Raccosta, Rodolfo Bianchi, Monty Caly, Cinzia Cindi, Malcolm Duff, Emilia Giuliano, Louis Walser
Soggetto: The protagonist, a former mercenary of the war in Honduras, lives in a small town near Tunis with the sole desire to forget his past of violence and

to marry his Joanna. The police do not lose sight of him, because "it is not possible" that Rolf has become normal again after those death experiences. Five of his former comrades show up again, led by John. They offer him, now a civilian pilot, the opportunity to transport a box of drugs to a certain place for a high fee. At first he refuses, then he accepts but only to destroy the deadly load of drugs. The five then retaliate by raping and killing his beloved Joanna. Rolf in turn swears revenge: he invites the five into a bush and, using his former guerrilla ploys, he eliminates them all with violent and brutal expedients. Then, exhausted and without any reason to live, he lets himself be handcuffed by the policemen who are looking for him.

Una tenera follia
Italia, 1977.
Regia di Ninì Grassia. Con Sonia Viviani, Saverio Vallone, Alex Damiani, Margie Newton, Pippo Baresi.

Cient'anne 1998
(Italia 1999, col 105)
Di Ninì Grassia
Con Gigi D'Alessio, Mario Merola, Gorge Hilton, Giorgio Mastrota, Cristina Parovel, Alessandra Monti (Mereghetti, 2002, cit).

Mr Replay (The Talented Mr Ripley)
by Anthony Minghella
prod William Horberg, Tom Sternberg per Mirage Enterprises/Timnick Film, *distr* Buena Vista international *sogg,* dal romanzo omonimo di Patricia Highsmith, *scen* Anthony Minghella, *dir fot*.John Seale, *mont* Walter Murch , *mus* Gabriel Yared, *scenog* Roy Walker *costum.* Ann Roth, Gary Jones.

Interpreti: Matt Demon (Tom Ripley), Gwyneth Paltrow, Jude Law (Dickie Greenleaf) Cate Blanchett, Philip Seymour Hoffmann, Jack Davenport, James Rebhorn, Sergio Rubini, Rosario Fiorello, Stefania Rocca, Ivano Marescotti, Philip Baker Hall, Lisa Eichhorn, Caterina Deregibus.

Il paradiso all'improvviso
Italia, 2003. Produzione Levante, distr. Medusa.
Regia di L. Pieraccioni.
Cast: Rocco Papaleo, Alessandro Haber, Angie Cepeda, Annamaria Barbera.

42 plus
Prod, Austria 2006
Regia Sabine Derflinger e Mogens Rukov
Con: Claudia Michelsen, Hulrick Tukur, Tobias Moretti, Petra Morzé, Vanessa Kruger, Jakob Mattschenz, Miriam Fiordeponti, Mario Giordano, Stefanie Dvorak, Ugo Conti.

The Angelo Rizzoli Award for Cinematographers

1st EDITION 1972

The Angelo Rizzoli award for cinematographers was established in 1972 by the Provincial Tourist Board of Naples and had the high patronage of the President of the Republic. On the occasion of the presentation of the award (Saturday October 7, 1972), the lawyer Luigi Torino, President of the Provincial Agency for Tourism, declared: the President of the Republic had the idea of honouring this award with his high patronage and with particular sensitivity, as Angelo Rizzoli left the memory of his initiatives that have contributed to bring the island among the most renowned international tourist resorts.

The award was given to Marco Ferreri's ***L'Udienza***, starring Enzo Jannacci, Claudia Cardinale and Ugo Tognazzi. Among the speakers: the solemn Pietro Nenni with his daughter Giuliana, Marco Ferreri, the publisher Bompiani, the sculptor Francesco Messina, Ugo Tognazzi with his wife Franca Bettoia, Andrea Rizzoli, the General Director of the De Biase Entertainment, the President of AGIS Gemini and Undersecretary Semeraro, representing the Minister for Tourism and Entertainment Badini-Confalonieri. On the morning of Sunday, October 8 a section of Via Roma, the main street of Lacco Ameno, was officially named after Angelo Rizzoli, and the bust-- the work of the sculptor Francesco Messina-- was inaugurated.

2nd and 3rd EDITONS 1973 / 1974
June 14-15-16, 1974

In the 1974 edition, two prizes were awarded, one for 1973, the year in which the event could not be held due to cholera, the other for 1974.
The titles in the running for 1973 were:
DELITTO MATTEOTTI by Florestano Vancini
LA VILLEGGIATURA by Marco Leto
LUDWIG by Luchino Visconti.
The jury, chaired by Leone Piccioni and composed of Rossella Falk, Ingrid Thulin, Alberto Bevilacqua, Alessandro Blasetti, Guglielmo Braghi, Franco Brusati, Domenico Meccoli, Giancarlo Menotti, Angelo Solmi, Vittorio Ricciuti, awarded the Prize to: LUDWIG by Luchino Visconti.
For 1974, the three works nominated for the Award included:
AMARCORD by Federico Fellini
IL PORTIERE DI NOTTE by Liliana Cavati
PANE E CIOCCOLATO by Franco Brusati. The jury was comprised of Leone Piccioni (President), Giannantonio Cibotto, Oreste Del Buono, Federico Fiasconi, Vittorio Gassman, Lisa Gastoni, Giovanni Grazzini, Sergio Leone, Sergio Lori, Alfredo Mezio and Leo Pestelli, designated as the winning film: AMARCORD by Federico Fellini . The award was collected by Giulietta Masina on behalf of her husband. Among those present: Ettore Scola, Claudia Cardinale, Miriam Bru, Barbara Bouchet, Giovanna Ralli, Franco Nero, Gillo Pontecorvo, Paola Quattrini, Ettore della Giovanna, the ladies Rizzoli-Carraro, Frida Franca Kasslater. Representing the government, the Undersecretary for Finance Giuseppe Amadei, the Prefect of Naples Amari and the Chief of Police Zamparelli. The

presenters were: Mariolina Cannuli and Lello Bersani.

4th EDITION
May 2-3-4, 1975
Film finalists:
PROFESSIONE REPORTER by Michelangelo Antonioni
FATTI DI GENTE PER BENE by Mauro Bolognini
C'ERAVAMO TANTO AMATI by Ettore Scola.Scola's film, however, was not presented.
The jury, chaired by Leone Piccioni and composed of Mariangela Melato, Guglielmo Braghi, Mario Cecchi Gori, Marcello Fondato, Renato Guttuso, Tullio Kezich, Michele Preisco, Domenico Rea, Paolo Ricci, Angelo Solmi, awarded the prize to Michelangelo Antonioni's PROFESSIONE REPORTER.
Two foreign films were also presented in this edition, awarded in their respective states:
LISICF by Yugoslavian director Tristo Papic
SHAZDZCK ENTEDIAB by Iranian director Houshang Golsaris.
Among the speakers: Giorgio Albertazzi, Anna Proclemer, Ottavia Piccolo, Barbara Bouchet, Philippe Leroy, Ettore Della Giovanna, Renzo Trionfiera, Paolo Valmarana....
The presenters were: Mariolina Cannuli and Lello Bersani.

5th EDITION
May 7-8-9, 1976
The jury was chaired by Giovanni Grazzini and made up of Monica Vitti, Gabriele Ferzetti, Liliana Cavani, Luigi Magni, Luigi Torino, Luigi Compagnone, Renato Ghiotto, Francesco Savio, Mario Stefanile

and Dario Zanelli. After viewing dozens of films, the jury narrowed its selections to some films, almost all of them under sequestration. Pietro Piccioni then proposed asking the Rizzoli Award of Ischia committee for extraterritoriality, as was done at the Venice Film Festival, to circumvent the obstacle of censorship. After intense debates, especially the one on the theme in "CENSURA; PERCHÉ?" the award was awarded to PIER PAOLO PASOLINI for all of his work. Pasolini's film, however, "SALO' E LE 120 GIORNATE DI SADOMA" could not be shown because it was seized. The Audience Award, FUNGO D'ARGENTO, offered by the Municipality of Lacco Ameno and awarded to AMICI MIEI, was refused in protest against the censorship and failure to see Pasolini's film.

The New Author Award went to Peter Del Monte's "IRENE IRENE". The presenters were: Gabriella Farinon and Renato Tagliani.

6th EDITION
May 6-7-8, 1977

Film finalists:
IL DESERTO DEI TARTARI by Valerio Zurlino
BRUTTI SPORCHI E CATTIVI by Ettore Scola
L'AGNESE VA A MORIRE by Giuliano Montaldo.
The jury, chaired by Leone Piccioni e made up of Virna Lisi, Alberto Arbasino, Carlo Ternari, Guglielmo Braghi, Tullio Kezich, Alberto Lattuada, Gianluigi Rondi, Angelo Solmi, Alberto Sordi and Luigi Torino, gave the award to *IL DESERTO DEI TARTARI* by Valerio Zurlino.

The Audience Award, FUNGO D'ARGENTO, was given to *BRUTTI SPORCHI E CATTIVI* by Ettore Scola.

In this edition an award was established for a young film director. The three movies that were pre-selected were:
UN CUORE SEMPLICE by Giorgio Ferrara
IO SONO UN AUTARCHICO by Nanni Moretti
STANDARD by Stefano Petruzzellis and the award was give to *UN CUORE SEMPLICE* by Giorgio Ferrara. Among the speakers: Maw Sidow, Giuliano Gemma, Monica Vitti, Paolo Villaggio, Marisa Mell, Liana Orfei, Duccio Tessari, Giancarlo Giannini, Iaja Fiastri, Eleonora Giorni, Massimo Girotti, Michele Placido, Peter Del Monte. The presenters were: Maria Giovanna Elmi e Lello Bersani.

7th EDITION
May 4-5-6, 1978

The film finalists were:
UNA GIORNATA PARTICOLARE by Ettore Scola,
IL GABBIANO by Marco Belloccio,
ALLEGRO MA NON TROPPO by Bruno Bozzetto. The jury gave the award to *UNA GIORNATA PARTICOLARE* by Ettore Scola. As for the award for a young Italian filmmaker, the three finalists were *ECCE BOMBO* by Nanni Moretti,
NON CONTATE SU DI NOI by Sergio Nuti, *HOMO SAPIENS* by Fiorella Mariani.
The award was given to *ECCE BOMBO* by Nanni Moretti.

8th – 9th EDITION
1979 and 1980

In 1980 the award was given to *CITTA' DELLE DONNE* was collected by the actress Donatella Damiani. The FUNGO D'ARGENTO was given to Luciano Odorisio for his film "*EDUCATORE AUTORIZZATO*".

10th EDITION
June 5-6-7, 1981

The film finalists:
RICOMINCIO DA TRE di Massimo Troisi,
TRE FRATELLI by Francesco Rosi, *IMMACOLATA E CONCETTA* by Salvatore Piscicelli.
The jury, chaired by Paolo Villaggio and composed of Alberto Bevilacqua, Franco Bruno, Monica Vitti, Luigi Torino, Gianluigi Rondi, Ugo Tognazzi, Roberto De Simone...gave the award to *RICOMINCIO DA TRE* by Massimo Troisi. The three finalists for the young Italian cinema, nominated for the FUNGO D'ARGENTO were: *IL FALCO E LA COLOMBA* by Fabrizio Lori, *A.A.A. GIOVANE DINAMICO MODERNO* by Salvatore Esposito,
STUPENDE LE MIE AMICHE by Alessandro Scalco. The jury chaired by Gianluigi Rondi gave the award to *IL FALCO E LA COLOMBA* by Fabrizio Lori,
The award for Best Actor was given to Massimo Troisi, the award for Best Actress to Ida di Benedetto, the best director to Francesca Rosi.
The Festival Cabaret Award was established at this edition and its finalists were: Gianni Ansaldi, Francesco Salvi, Mauro Di Francesco and Paolo Rossi. The jury, made up of Paolo Villaggio, I Gatti di Vicolo Miracoli and Diego Abatantuono awarded Maurizio Di Crescenzo.
The presenters were: Maria Giovanna Elmi and Lello Bersani.

11th EDITION
May 6-7-8, 1982

The film finalists were:
BOROTALCO by Carlo Verdone,
PISO PISELLO by Peter Del Monte,
AD OVEST DI PAPERINO by Alessandro Benvenuti. The jury chaired by Leone Piccioni and was composed of Massimo Fichera, Valerio Caprara, Armando Trovatoli, Fulvio Lucidano, Claudia Cardinale, Edith Bruck, Luigi Torino, Paolo Valmorana, Franco Rosi, Luigi Proietti, and gave the award to *PISO PISELLO* di Peter Del Monte. Il FUNGO D'ARGENTO awarded by the audience went instead to *BOROTALCO* by Carlo Verdone. The award for Best Actor was given to Alberto Sordi, and for Best Actress to Eleonora Giorgi, Best Debutant Actor to Beppe Grillo. Other awards were given to Liv Ulmann, Valeria D'Obici, Alessandro Haber, Mario Cecchi Gori...Among the speakers were Angelo Rizzoli junior and his wife Eleonora Giorni, Alberto Sordi, Leopoldo Mastelloni, Giuliano Gemma, Fabio Testi, Mariangela Melato, Ugo Tognazzi...The presenters were: Daniela Poggi e Lello Bersani.

12th EDITION
May 26-27-28, 1983

The film finalists were:
COLPIRE AL CUORE by Gianni Amelio,
IO, CHIARA E LO SCURO by Maurizio Ponzi,
LA NOTTE DI SAN LORENZO by P.e V. Taviani. The jury, chaired by Antonio Girelli and composed of Filiberto Bandini, Guglielmo Braghi, Callisto Cosulich, Vittorio Cottafi, Claudio G.Fava, Vittorio Pellegrino, Michele Prisco, Anna Proclemer, Nino Manfredi, gave the award to *COLPIRE AL CUORE*

by Gianni Amelio. The FUNGO D'ARGENTO was given by the audience to *IO, CHIARA E LO SCURO* by Maurizio Ponzi. The three finalists for original movies were: *ANDANDO PER FESTE* by Nino Russi, *FUORI DAL GIORNO* by Paolo Bologna, *HERENGARD* by Emilio Greco. The movie that received the award was *ANDANDO PER FESTE* by Nino Russi. The award for Best Actor went to Francesco Nuti, and for Best Actress to Mariangela Melato. The speakers were: Ida Di Benedetto, Lello Arena, Jenni Tamburi, Philippe Leroy, Lina Sastri, Domenico Rea, Carlo Lizzani, Milena Vukovic, Mariangela Melato, Nino Manfredi, Giuliana De Sio…The presenters were: Simona Izzo e Lello Bersani.

13th EDITION
From May 31 to June 2, 1984

The film finalists were:
BALLANDO BALLANDO by Ettore Scola,
BIANCA by Nanni Moretti,
GITA SCOLASTICA by Pupi Avati.
The jury was chaired by Iaja Fiastri and was composed of Franco Bruno, Franco Busati, Valerio Caprara, Carmine Cianfarani, Giuliana De Sio, Fernaldo Di Giammatteo, Carlo Lizzani, Enrico Montesano, Vittorio Pellegrino. The jury gave the award to *BALLANDO BALLANDO* by Ettore Scola. The Audience Award, il FUNGO D'ARGENTO, went to *GITA SCOLASTICA* by Pupi Avati. The award for Best Actress went to Monica Scattini, for Best Actor to Ugo Tognazzi. For the young cinema, the LUIGI TORINO award, there were three finalists: *FLIRT* by Roberto Russo, *DENTRO CASA* by Francesca De Chiara, *LA VERITA' NON SI DICE* by Maria Bosio.

The pre-selected film was *FLIRT* by Roberto Russo. Among the speakers: Giovanni Grazzini, Luigi Magni, Armando Trovatoli, Carlo Verdone, Giacomo Rizzo, Lello Arena, Imma Piro, il Prefetto Boccia, the president of Cinecittà Antonio Manca. The presenters were: Jenny Tamburo e Lello Bersani.

14th EDITION
July 11-12-13, 1985

The film finalists were:
CARMEN by Francesco Rosi,
KAOS by the Fratelli Traviani,
NOI TRE by Pupi Avati.
The jury was chaired by Leone Piccioni and was composed of Barbara De Rossi, Claudio Carraba, Callisto Cosulich, Fabio Ferzetti, Marcello Fondato, Tullio Kezich, Luigi Magni, Vittorio Pellegrino, Luigi Proietti, Mario Cecchi Gori. The jury gave teh award to CARMEN by Francesco Rosi. The three finalists for the Italian young cinema were: *YBRIS* by Gavino Ledda, *CHI MI AIUTA* by Valerio Zecca, *IL MISTERO DEL MORCA* by Marco Mattolini. Il FUNGO D'ARGENTO went to *CHI MI AIUTA* by Valerio Zecca. The award for Best Actor went to CHI MI AIUTA by Omero Antonutti, while that for Best Actress to Enrica Maria Modugno. The Stampa Europea award went to: VINCENTE ANTONIO PINEDA (Spain) GIDEON BACHMAN (England) MARCELLE PADOVANI (France).
Among the speakers: Ugo e Ricky Tognazzi, Tony Musante, Edwige Fenech, Luciano De Crescenzo, Ida Di Benedetto, Jaia Fiastri, ArmandoTrovajoli, Enrika Blanc, Enrico Vanzina, Eriprando Visconti, Natasha Havey.
 The presenters were: Jenny Tamburo e Alberto Lionello.

Printed in Great Britain
by Amazon